DONALD DAVIE
Collected Poems 1970-1983

CARCANET NEW PRESS / Manchester
MID NORTHUMBERLAND ARTS GROUP / Ashington
UNIVERSITY OF NOTRE DAME PRESS / Notre Dame, Indiana

Certain of these poems appeared, variously, in the following magazines: *PN Review, Occident, The American Scholar, The Sewanee Review, Sequoia, Vanderbilt Poetry Review, Agenda, Inquiry, The Times Literary Supplement, The Cambridge Review, The Threepenny Review, The Irish Times.* The writing of some of them was facilitated by grants from the Simon Guggenheim Foundation, and the Rockefeller Foundation. I am glad to record my gratitude to each of these institutions and journals. D.D.

First published in England in 1983 by
Carcanet New Press Ltd
210 Corn Exchange Buildings
Manchester M4 3BQ
and
Mid Northumberland Arts Group
Town Hall, Ashington
Northumberland

U S Edition 1983 by
University of Notre Dame Press
Notre Dame, Indiana 46556

ISBN 0-85635-462-7 (Carcanet)
ISBN 0-904790-30-4 (MidNAG)
ISBN 0-268-00745-4 (Notre Dame)

Printed in England by Short Run Press Ltd, Exeter

COLLECTED POEMS
1970-1983

TO PETER DAVIE
my grandson

A composition of Grace's
And Mark's, dear Peter, may you
Be everything I say you,
And always bear the traces
Of your nativity:
A man of mark; a pretty
Anthology of graces.

CONTENTS

A POEM OF THE 1960s

PILATE

The chief of the civil administration
                        of the occupying power reflects
in the forty-five minutes he allows himself each morning
over a cigarette for the world to
                        re-achieve its third dimension daily
(Saving shadows and memories
                        vine on his nerves' snapped trellis):

'Between the judicial and
                        the nervously judicious
the best of Rome bleeds
                        into the sands of Judaea.'

The best? Ho-hum. The keeping up of standards
(The right ones, Roman), how it sustained him once!

The harm it does him,
                        the practice of severity
which someone has to do, he
                        knows. He knows it. He is bad at it
in his own estimation, but
some one has to and
                        whether in good faith
is no problem:
                        You keep yourself busy,
too many cases in too little time and such
scruple as there is time for.

Aggressive-pusillanimous, the harm it
did him, and perhaps it does
                        any one is known to him, wherein
virtue perhaps. He has
nothing to show to be proud of
                        from his H.Q. years but rare
acts of intellectual
                        brutality: 'This is no good . . .'
'No, I will not . . .'
                        His

skills were not of that order
                    but being of no account
until perverted, they
                    patiently were perverted:
skills to the end of inspiring
emulation, that
                    ingenious artifice
called 'leadership' (and what
an orator he might have been, a
poet even) were
                    perverted to other ends,
to the end of sitting in judgement.

It is the lion of Judah is all claws.
Caiaphas has the style of the officer-class.

Skills to the end of finding
out short-circuited
                    in finding fault, he
knows. He knows it. He is bad at it.

But if it is all he finds with
certainty? The *pax
Romana* is worth something. His
                    wish to be lenient mimes
a charity he dare not
                    not respect but knows he
cannot profess.
                    He does not
in any event perceive
that for these responsible scruples
                    the *soi-disant* King of the Jews
has very much more forbearance
than His accusers.

THE SHIRES (1974)

BEDFORDSHIRE

Bunyan, of course. But Potton it was, or Sandy,
Threaded on the Cambridge road, that showed
Dissenting nineteenth-century demureness
In a brick chapel. I have never known
What to do with this that I am heir to.

My daughter-in-law has studied for her thesis
The Protestant Right in France between the wars,
l'Association Sully. Bedfordshire
Might nurse an English counterpart of that:

Our swords for Calvin and the Winter Queen,
The ancient frail collaborating Marshal!

BERKSHIRE
for Michael Hamburger

Don't care for it.
                    We talked of syntax and
synecdoche, the various avant-gardes,
their potencies, their puerilities.
And, Michael, one we knew
in Reading, he approved such conversations;
crippled and dying he contrived occasions
when they could come about. And yet he
felt (we knew) not scepticism, rather . . .
oh certainly not scepticism, rather
an eager, a too eager warmth in him
starved for a lack of body in that talk.

In his last months I stood him up for supper.
That night I should have stayed with him I stayed
talking with Christopher Middleton in town.

So nowadays as the biscuit-factory flies
past the train-window and announces Reading,
I keep my head down.

BUCKINGHAMSHIRE

A thin green salient aimed at the heart of London,
The trains run in and out of Baker Street.

Chalfont St Giles, Chalfont St Peter, Fenny
And Stony Stratford breathe again. The old
A6, the clamorous ditch we edge along,
Ribbons in evening sunlight south to Bletchley.

To west and east the motorways draw off
Poisons that clogged this artery. Abandoned
Transport-cafés blink at the weedy asphalt;
An old white inn by a copse-side yawns and stretches.

CAMBRIDGESHIRE
'An air that kills'—Housman

Housman came, savage recluse,
Lover of boys. 'To be sure,
That also I endure,
    yet not from there
Blows into Whewell's Court
    an air that kills.'

Came wincing Gray: 'Why that
Libertine over the way,
Smart of Pembroke, should
    have had the luck
    of running mad
Is more than I can say.'

Smart stares at William Blake:
'Mad? Mad as a refuge
    merely from Locke?
Shame on the subterfuge!
    Let the wind pluck
Your wits astray, *then* talk!'

And Blake: 'I accept the reproof.
Better be sane like Housman
Than under Bedlam's roof,
Self-soiled, wind-plucked. And yet
    I think it's not
    an airless place?'

Smart, Gray, all of them, look:
The face of Harold Monro!
'An air that kills? At all
    events an air!'
Tuneless, he growls from Caius
    in his despair.

CHESHIRE

A lift to the spirit, when everything fell into place!
So that was what those ruined towers remained from:
Engine-houses, mills. Our Pennine crests
Had not been always mere unfettered space.

Not quite the crests, just under them. The high
Cloughs, I learned in the history-lesson, had
Belted the earliest mills, they had connived
With history then, then history passed them by.

His savage brunt and impetus, one survives it?
Finding it all unchanged and the windowless mill
Between Wincle and Congleton silent and staring, I found
The widow's weeds restorative and fit.

And Mr Auden, whom I never knew,
Is dead in Vienna. A post-industrial landscape
He celebrated often, and expounded
How it can bleakly solace. And that's true.

CORNWALL

(Treasure Island)

Cornwall, the unreality
of Cornwall:

hull down, the mobile homes
are shelling the Bristol Channel

which fights right back! Storm-lanterns
swing in the black
wind, and tomorrow
perspex and fibre-glass
will slosh about in the eddies.

Cornwall, the fabulous wreckers
of Cornwall: novelists.

A county in Bermuda,
that unreality also.
It was a literary Empire.

Black Jack Pendennis has
been out again. To a lonely
inn upon Bodmin Moor
etcetera, on a wild
October night
etcetera.

Different for the Cornish,
it must be. But for us
Lancashire and Yorkshire
interlopers who
run curio-shops on the quay
it has, as an arena
for growing old in, one
desolate advantage:
it cannot be believed in.

Black patches on both eyes . . .

CUMBERLAND

I tend to suppose the part I know least
Of England is the north-west.

A honeymoon in the Lake District
Is conventional matter-of-fact;

And ours was the winter of '45!
On ghyll and yew-tree grove

And packhorse-bridge, the blowtorch air
Was singeing the nostril-hair;

Snow that had lain deep for weeks
Fantasticated our walks;

And Rydal Water to our tread
Rang, till Helvellyn heard.

Exalted by love, in wintry rigours
Unlikely Cumberland rages

Thus in my memories. North-west,
I know you least, or best?

DERBYSHIRE

We never made it. Time and time again
Sublimity went unexamined when
We turned back home through Winster, lacking heart
For walking further. Yet the Romantic part
Of Via Gellia, where it dives through chasms
To Ashbourne, is historic; there, short spasms
Of horror once in many a heaving breast
Gave Derbyshire a dreadful interest.

And I too was Romantic when I strode
Manfully, aged 12, the upland road.

Only the name of 'Via Gellia' jarred;
It seemed to mean a classical boulevard
With belvederes at intervals. I swelled
My little chest disdainfully, I 'rebelled'!

DEVONSHIRE

Discharged upon the body of the world
   Drake, Hawkins, all that semen
   Has left no stain! Instead
   The disblitzed Plymouth: first
Violin to squeal the eunuch's part
   Well-planned, a work of art.

We run through a maze of tunnels for our meat
   As rats might; underpass,
   Walkway, crash-barrier lead
   Our willing steps, as does
The questionnaire that we shall be so kind
   As to complete (unsigned)

Between North Road and Paddington. Drake's Circus
   Proffers the hoops the trained
   Corpulent animals are
   Glad to jump through. Drake,
This is the freedom that you sailed from shore
   To save us for?

DORSET

John Fowles's book, *The French Lieutenant's Woman*:
'A grand ebullient portrait certainly'
Of Thomas Hardy's country, where however
I would not strike such sparkles. Slow and vocal
Amber of a burring baritone
My grandad's voice, not Hardy's, is what stays

Inside me as a slumbrous apogee,
Meridional altitude upon
Pastoral England's longest summer day.

O golden age! Bee-mouth, and honeyed singer!

COUNTY DURHAM

Driving up from Tees-side
The first and only time,
I had been there before;
I might have been in Goldthorpe.

My cousin kept a shop
For baby-linen in Goldthorpe;
Doing the same in Brighouse
An aunt went out of her mind.

But mostly, visible beauty
Intruded on a coal-field
So little, one was not
Unsettled by its absence.

Coal-field! A term like tundra,
Rain-forest, *karst*, savannah;
A humanly created
Topographical constant.

Indelible! Let rosebay
Willow herb, fiery emblem,
Push as it will, let the pits
Close, there will still be Goldthorpe.

I am told at the miners' gala
They bear green boughs and, Prince-
Bishop, a Lord of Misrule
Preaches in your cathedral.

And I am supposed to be
Delighted by that survival?
My Lord, your Lord of Misrule
Ruled, and rules, in Goldthorpe.

ESSEX

Names and things named don't match
Ever. This is not
A plethora of language,
But language's condition;

Sooner or later the whole
Cloth of the language peels off
As wallpaper peels from a wall,
However it 'hangs together'.

With Essex moreover the case is
Especially grievous: hope,
Disappointment, fatuous shocks
And surprises pattern the fabric.

Constable's country merits
Better than I can give it
Who have unfinished business
There, with my own failures.

GLOUCESTERSHIRE
for Charles and Brenda

Not architecture, not
(Good heavens!) city-planning,
But a native gift for townscape
Appears to have distinguished
The pre-industrial English.

Parochialism therefore,
Though of a Tuscan kind,
Discovers in the practice
Of this one homely art
The measure of *civiltà*.

A laudable Little England
Grounded on this conviction
Would fortify the Cotswolds,
Adopting as its tribal
Metropolis Chipping Camden.

HAMPSHIRE

'Our argute voices vied among the bracken.'
    My sixth-form prize from the North
Was Ronald Bottrall's *Festivals of Fire*,
    My own precocious choice.

A chaste young sailor (one thing I was not
    Precocious at was sex),
Abruptly, two years later, I pronounced
    This verse to a willowy Wren.

An educated girl, she recognized
    The bracken where we stood
Alone together in a woodland ride,
    And took 'argute' on trust.

Past that same wood near Wickham, that same year,
    My nineteenth autumn, I
Rode the country bus from Winchester
    To 'Collingwood' at Fareham.

Alone I'd spent my week-end's leave upon
    St Catherine's Hill, upon
Wolvesey Castle, the Cathedral Close;
    Seen the Round Table, doubtful.

All the South Country that I knew from books!
    Joining the Navy meant
My first time south to London, south from there
    Into my element:

Verses and books, 'argute' and Camelot.
I could correct that Hampshire, but shall not.

HEREFORDSHIRE

At Hay, or near it, 1944
on winter leave, and walking through the moonlight
the country roads with Gavin Wright, I sealed
with a prompt fear the classical commonplace:
'As one who walks alone at night and fears
each brigand bush, each clump a nest of spears . . .'
I read that later, out of Juvenal.

A classical region, then? I think so, yes.
Though those were the Welsh Marches, it was not
classical Europe that we beat the bounds of;
barbarians indeed were at our doors
but not round there where, in a world at war,
with atavistic Englishness I saw
the black Black Mountains menacing our acres.

HERTFORDSHIRE

Was it, I wondered, some freak
of earth or just bad technique
    on the builder's part that made
    the pavement blocks before
    our friends' house hump and crack?
Could we, as our city shoes slipped
think Hertfordshire equipped,
    as Kent and Surrey were not,

thus to resist the encroaching
    concrete apron of London?
No hope of that, alas!
An aspiring middle-class
    could however, we saw,
    make a humanly touching thing
    out of a suburb. It was
not wholly anonymous ground
on which they moved around,
    if it could mutiny thus
    in an Anglo-Jewish enclave
    between Finchley and Barnet.
Displacement and decay
provided for, brought into play
    by a prudent builder ensure
    that, suddenly dying, we leave
    our friends with something to say.

HUNTINGDONSHIRE

Italian prisoners of war still haunted
    The Huntingdon we quartered
For flats to rent, untimely family
    A student's grant supported.

Many such families, then. The shaking frames
    Of a shared memory feature
A man from Pembroke with his Serbian bride,
    A sexless rawboned creature.

They lived, they said, in a jacked, abandoned bus.
    We wondered: Could they suckle,
Those flattened breasts? And the fingers! Labour Camps
    Had broken every knuckle.

What has become of them? Foolish to ask. But to couples
    We sometimes meet, we assign a
Not dissimilar past: our Roman host
    Has a Polish wife with *angina*.

Huntingdon's bard, androgynous William Cowper,
    Announced it to us all:
That Simoïs and Mincio, like Ouse,
    Sucked down his garden-wall.

KENT

Chatham was my depot,
Chatty Chatham, 'chatty'
Meaning squalid. So it
Was, the little town
One trundled to out of London
As to a dead-end England.

Of course I knew this was
To get things upside-down;
Still, so it proved for some
Soon after, in E-Boat Alley.

LANCASHIRE

My father was born in Horton
In Ribblesdale—the highest
Signal-box in England
He'd say, but he was biased.

Though Horton is in Yorkshire,
The Ribble flows to the west.
I have imagined that river
With awful interest:

Dark gullies, sobbing alders
Must surely mark its course;
It rolls and rounds its boulders
With more than natural force.

For down that sombre valley
(I knew, without being told)
The famous Lancashire witches
Had long ago taken hold,

And a troop of Catholic gentry
Mustered from manors near
Rode hopelessly to Preston
To join the Chevalier.

Liverpool, Manchester, Salford
I've seen, and felt oppressed;
But Clitheroe's haunted river
I've never put to the test.

Should anyone taunt me with this,
The sneer's well merited.
But I pray you, remember my father—
The fault's inherited.

LEICESTERSHIRE

From a view to a kill in pursuit
Of what can't fill the belly
May do for hunting the fox;
But I. A. Richards on Shelley
Was an obfuscating splendour.

Equally there in Leicester
I listened to the aureate
Archaic tongue of Blunden,
Who through his spell as laureate
Of Oxford smiled and was speechless.

Perhaps the Leicester Poetry
Society is still calling
Its week-end schools together;
It's my fault if I've fallen
Out of touch with its sponsors.

At Loughborough, I remember,
A man too little regarded
(Dead since), V. C. Clinton-
Baddeley afforded
Several views of Yeats.

LINCOLNSHIRE
for Kathleen Wilson

Simpering sideways under a picture-hat
Gainsborough Lady, every Odeon
Or Gaumont of the 'thirties knew her well.

Those British films she regally inclined
To sponsor were, I see now, laying claim
To suavities like Gainsborough the painter's.

Tricked by the name, though, I for years envisaged
Milady at her town in Lincolnshire;
Gainsborough, a sort of Tunbridge Wells.

Beau Nash was there, Beau Brummel took the waters.
If films were shot there (not the ones we saw
Oddly enough), they were demure and tasteful.

The place to go to see the Gainsborough Lady,
As I remember, was the Globe in New Street.
Cousin Kathleen, did you ever go there?

I think you may have done, going or coming
From grandmother's in Day Street. If you did,
Were you, like me, seduced by the genteel?

Easy to see you might be. There were rough
Diamonds all about us; Barnsley-born,
In us some mincing was forgivable.

In Louth that Tory stronghold, in the trilled
Late light on the wolds, a false refinement irks
As not in grimy Gainsborough or Scunthorpe.

MIDDLESEX

Germans, she said, were sometimes independent;
Her countrymen were all for package-tours,

A girl from Wembley Stadium serving beers
In a Greek bar. A maxiskirt from Bristol
Hawked prints on the Acropolis; from Chepstow
Another served us in a coffee-bar.
Our age-group is dependent, but not theirs.

Temporary drop-outs or true wives
To young and struggling Greeks, they do us more
Credit than we deserve, their timid parents.

The longer loop their Odysseys, the more
Warmly exact the Ithakas they remember:
Thus, home she said was Middlesex, though Wembley
I should have named, indifferently, as 'London'.

MONMOUTHSHIRE
for Doreen

The colonist's 'they' that needs no antecedent;
And as self-evident for the colonized—
Both mouths remorseless. For the Silurist
Self-styled, for Henry Vaughan, both
      Unthinking pronouns missed
The peaceful point three hundred years ago.

Anglo-Welsh: that mixture took and held
Through centuries. My dear wife, we endorsed it:
Our sons are a quarter Welsh if they care to think so.
Our brother-in-law was happy, when the Sappers'
      Reunion was in Chepstow,
To gossip with old comrades of Cawnpore.

NORFOLK

An arbitrary roll-call
Of worthies: Nelson, Paine,
Vancouver, Robert Walpole.

Vancouver, stolid Dutchman
Born at Lynn, forgotten;
Too much the flogging captain.

Walpole: heaven-high smell of
Whitewash on tainted beef,
Piquant in learning's nostril.

(Unprincipled, vindictive,
All that Pope said, and worse
Confirmed, and spelt as virtue.)

But Nelson and mysterious
Tom Paine, baleful in Thetford,
Napoleonic portents . . .

Who answers for the double
Aspect of genius, arcing
From Corsica or Norfolk?

NORTHAMPTONSHIRE

King's Cliffe, in the evening: that Northampton stone
As fine as Cotswold, and more masculine . . .

Turpin on wheels, my long-lost self that rode
Southward the Great North Road, and had

This bourne in mind, that night was disconcerted:
Youth hostel, yes; also a sort of shrine.

To William Law! Well, later on I learned
To gut that author for my purposes.

Questions remain, however. William Law,
Saint of the English Church . . . And what is sainthood?

Some leading questions must be answered soon,
Lead where they will, scared schoolboy, where they will!

NORTHUMBERLAND

'I hear Aneurin number the dead'—(Brigg Flatts)

Johnson's pentameters, nailed by the solid *ictus*;
'Felt percussion of the marching legions.'

Late excavations on the Wall report
The garrisons lived there in their excrement;

Centurions with their centuries, some thousands
—A decimal system drills to a count of ten—
Barked to a halt when Aneurin numbered the dead.

The laboured mole dilapidates, surmounted
By barrel-chests, Aegean or Cymric metres.

NOTTINGHAMSHIRE

Rosebay willow herb pushing
through patches of old slag
in the curtains of driving rain
obscured the Major Oak.

Or else (our steam was blurring
the windows of the Hillman)
it was our being hounded
out of doors that felled
the last tall stands of Sherwood.

Robin of Locksley, Guy
of Gisborne, and the Sheriff

of Nottingham had been dapples
under my mother's smiles
all down the glades of boyhood.

But now she could take no more
of us, and of our baby.

In the country of *Sons and Lovers*
we think we know all too much
about the love of mothers.

Angry and defiant,
rash on industrial waste,
the rosebay willow herb
is, of all the flowers
she taught me, one I remember.

OXFORDSHIRE

'Start such a fire in England, Master Ridley,
As shall not be put out'—the coupled martyrs
That Oxford steers by in its Morris Minors
Fried for a quibble in Scripture or Canon Law!

Saints we remember, must we remember martyrs?
Baptists though we were, I knew from childhood
Latimer's words, and knew the fire he meant:
Godly work, the pious Reformation.

Crucifixions! Hideousness of burning,
Sizzle of fats, the hideous martyrdoms:
Palach consumed in Prague, a human torch;
A Saigon Buddhist, robe a more lambent saffron;

Dead for a country, dead for a Constitution
(Allende, in his mouth the emptied chamber
Of prompt and fluent deputies), were these
Crucifixions? They were suicides.

'Martyrs may seek their death, but may not seize it . . .'
Fine scruples, fine distinctions! Can there be
Any too fine for fine-toned Oxford, in
The smell of roast meat and the glare of torches?

RUTLAND
for George Dekker

Joke county, smallest in England.
But I remember distinctly, more than once,
Swinging the car at the bend by the railway yards
In Oakham, Rutland's county town. The last
Time was to see—I think you remember, George,
For your own reasons—paintings by my old
Friend, Bill Partridge. Dead now. Had you noticed?

How heavy that weighs, how wide the narrowest shire!

SHROPSHIRE

This has to be for my school-chum Billy Greaves
Who surfaced out of the past two years ago,
Breaking his journey to Fiji off one of his leaves;
He spoke to me by phone from San Francisco.

If we had met (we agreed upon 'next time'),
Would reminiscences have turned to Clun,
Clungunford, Clunbury, and Housman's rhyme?
('Quietest places,' he called them, 'under the sun.')

Possibly not; though once we wore out brake-blocks
Coasting from Wenlock Edge. And days gone by
Furnish a line of talk that's orthodox
For chance-met class-mates under a foreign sky.

Things change. Gone now the troublesome chores of Empire
That might earn such indulgences. We've seen,

Billy and I, our fractious nation tire
Too soon of holding Suva for the Queen.

Our parents at their tennis-club . . . A high
Lob in the last light hangs like Nemesis
On 1912! Deceived, my father's eye
Foresees the easy smash that he will miss.

Still, I'd quite like it, Billy, if you could
Recall for me above what gravelly flats
In what fly-haunted stream it was, we stood
In the weak light, pyjama-ed, swiping at bats.

SOMERSET

Antennae of the race,
'the damned and despised *literati* . . .'

Just how, she wanted to know
(swinging a shopping-bag
from Bridgwater), could
William Pitt have depended
for his intelligence on
a coterie in Racedown:
Coleridge and Southey, Wordsworth?

Big as a mule, a stag
through hedgerows down from Exmoor,
wall-eyed, nostrils flaring,
could not intrude more rudely
upon an *avant-garde*
seminar in the Quantocks.

STAFFORDSHIRE

The jaunty style of Arnold Bennett's 'Card' . . .

From years ago I call to mind my father,
flushed and uncertain, stalling time after time
a borrowed car in Newcastle-under-Lyme,

who had sung as a young man, 'I was one of the knuts'.

SUFFOLK

Something gone, something gone out with Nelson,
With him or by him. Something in its place:
A Dynamo! Broke of the Shannon takes,
Crippled in his retirement, a sedate
Pride in totting up the butcher's bills
Of single-ship engagements, finds his own
(His head still singing from an American cutlass)
The bloodiest yet. Audacity of Nelson
Sired Broke and calloused him; Jane Austen's hero,
Honourable, monogamous and sober,
Gunnery-expert, servant of the State,
His small estate was somewhere here, in Suffolk.
A better image should be found for it.

My education gave me this bad habit
Of reading history for a hidden plot
And finding it; invariably the same one,
Its fraudulent title always, 'Something Gone'.

Gainsborough might have painted him, with his
Wife and children and a sleek retriever
(Thomas Gainsborough, born at Sudbury)
In a less glaring light, a truer one.

SURREY

'In yonder grave a Druid lies'—('Ode on the Death of Thomson')

Who now reads Thomson or Collins?

'Conifer country of Surrey',
wrote Betjeman, 'approached through
remarkable wrought-iron gates.'

No missing the affection
there, nor the observation.

But on the Thames at Richmond
less tenderly, an eye for
the general more than the pungent
had lifted it to grandeur:

'Suspend the dashing oar.'

SUSSEX

Chiddingly, pronounced
Chiddinglye: the oast-house
Received us with warm brick,
A croquet-lawn, and squirrels.

And like the transatlantic
Visitors we were,
Our self-congratulations
And charmed response were fervent.

The most poeticized
Of English counties, and
An alien poet's eye,
Mine, there to endorse it.

We had to pinch ourselves
To know we knew the rules

Of cricket played on the green.
Our boy will never learn them.

'Brain-drain' one hears no more of,
And there's no loss. There is
Another emigration:
Draining away of love.

WARWICKSHIRE
for Roy Fisher

Eye on the object, eye on the congeries
Of objects, eye on the scene
with figures of course, eye on the scene with figures,
delivers us Birmingham. Who is to say it squints?

And yet Spaghetti Junction on the M
6 is, shall we say,
a comparable alternative solution
(to a problem of traffic-flow
in several ways at once on several levels)
to the Piazza d'Aracoeli. Shall we
say that much or in
the Shakespeare country can we? If the tongue
writhes on the foreign syllables, it shows
small relish for your balder registrations,

intent, monocular, faithful.

WESTMORLAND

Kendal . . . Shap Fell! Is that in Westmorland?
For one who espouses the North,
I am hazy about it, frankly. It's a chosen
North of the mind I take my bearings by,
A stripped style and a wintry;

As on Shap Fell, the only time I was there,
Wind cutting over and snowflakes beginning to sail
Slantwise across, on haulage vans clashing their gears
And me who had walked from Glasgow.

An end-of-October taste, a shade too late
For the right full ripeness. The style is decadent almost,
Emaciated, flayed. One knows such shapes,
Such minds, such people, always in need of a touch
Of frost, not to go pulpy.

WILTSHIRE

A brutally sheared-off cliff
Walling a cutting between
Barnsley and Doncaster is
The Railway Age in essence.

More cliffs, the hanging gardens
Of gossamer soot as the train
Creeps into Liverpool Street—
This too is in keeping.

But also consider the bugle
And stage-coach clatter silenced;
The beep and vroom of the Daimler
Unheard, and on the chalk

The human beetle rising
And falling for hours in the silence,
The distance: Jude the Obscure
Approaching, on Salisbury Plain.

WORCESTERSHIRE
for Doreen.

The best way in (not that I've checked the map)
Might be from West by North, as once we came
After a drive through spooky Radnor Forest
Where you had sat upon a picnic rug
And wept and wept. I laboured into verse
My sense of that, and made no sense at all.

Maria Theresa, I addressed you as,
Imperial sorrow. God knows what I meant
By that, or thought I meant. If I could not
Make you Fair Austria then, I shall not now;
But spin you down, down by whatever stages
Wise maps might tell me, into the blossoming plains.

Feed you with apples, stay you with flagons, Empress!
Acre on acre of orchards of Worcester Pearmains!

YORKSHIRE
Of Graces

The graces, yes—and the airs! To airs and graces
Equally the West Riding gave no houseroom
When I was young. Ballooning and mincing airs
Put on in the 'down there' of England! I was
Already out of place in the heraldic
Cities of the Midlands—Warwick, Leicester, the South . . .

   —And therefore it is a strain, thinking of Brough
   And Appleby gone from King John to a Frenchman
   For dirty work done on the roads of Poitou.

This helps me—not to pipe like your reed, Bunting,
Master of Northern stops—but to remember,
Never quite well enough, Kirkby Stephen
By Aisgill on to Hawes, to Aysgarth, Askrigg,

The narrow dale past a hump of broken stones.
Slant light out of Lancashire burnished the fell.

Alix, Kate, Eleanor, Anne—Angevin names—
You were not my hopscotch-mates; but Rhoda,
Thelma and Mona. Enormous their mottled
Fore-arms drove flat-irons later, strove with sheets
In old steam-laundries. There the Saxons queened it
No less—the Elfridas, Enids, many Hildas.

Ladies, ladies! Shirley or Diane or . . .
Which of you girls will be mine? Which of you all
In my dishonourable dreams sits smiling
Alone, at dusk, and knowledgeably sidelong,
Perched on a heap of stones, where 'Dangerous' says
The leaning board, on a green hill south of Brough?

Where is the elf-queen? Where the beldam Belle Dame?
Feyness of the North, kelpie of some small beck
In a swale of marble swirls over Durham,
Irrigates Elmet, combs the peat in Ewden.
And I have no faith in that: *le fay* thinned out
Into a pulse in the grass, St Winifred.

Eleanor rather, Alix, ladies of Latins,
I call you down. (And Mary, Mother of Heaven?)
Justice and Prudence (Prue, a name not given
North of the Trent), Courage, and Temperance were
Your erudite names, mothers of Latin earth.
What *royaume* of earth, elf-queen, did you sway ever?

Charites or *Gratiae*, the Graces,
Lemprière says, 'presided over kindness',
Each dam in her own kind fructive. Only two.
(Three came later.) Two: *Hegemone*, the Queen,
And *Auxo*, Increase. Queen of Elfland, in what
Assize did you sit, what increase ever foster?

Now every girl has this elvish admixture.
Thomas of Ercildoune, what you dreamed of once

Fogs every brae-side: lank black the hair hangs down,
The curves of the cheek are hollow and ravaged.
Their womanhood a problematic burden
To them and their castrated mates, they go past.

I have a Grace. Whether or no the Muses
Patronize me, I have a Grace in my house
And no elf-lady. Queen she is called, and Increase,
Though late-come, straitened, of a Northern Province.

IN THE STOPPING TRAIN
& OTHER POEMS (1977)

FATHER, THE CAVALIER

I have a photograph here
   In California where
You never were, of yourself
   Riding a white horse. And
The horse and you are dead
   Years ago, although
Still you are more alive
   To me than anyone living.

As for the horse: an ugly
   Wall-eyed brute, apparently
Biddable though, for I cannot
   Believe you were ever much of
A horseman. That all came late:
   Suddenly, in your forties,
Learning to ride! A surrogate
   Virility, perhaps . . .

For me to think so could not
   Make you any more
Alive than you have been here,
   Open-necked cricket-shirt
And narrow head, behind
   The pricked ungainly ears
Of your white steed—all these
   Years, unnoticed mostly.

THE HARROW

Unimaginable beings—
Our own dead friends, the dead
Notabilities, mourned and mourning,
Hallam and Tennyson . . . is it
Our loss of them that harrows?

Or is it not rather
Our loss of images for them?

The continued being of Claude
Simpson can be imagined.
We cannot imagine its mode.

Us too in this He harrows. It is not
Only on Easter Saturday
That it is harrowing
To think of Mother dead,
To think, and not to imagine.

He descended into—
Not into Hell but
Into the field of the dead
Where he roughs them up like a tractor
Dragging its tray of links.

Up and down the field, a tender bruising,
A rolling rug of iron, for the dead
Them also, the Virtuous Pagans
And others, He came, He comes
On Easter Saturday and

Not only then He comes
Harrowing them—that they,
In case they doubted it, may
Quicken and in more
Than our stale memories stir.

THE DEPARTED

They see his face!

Live in the light of . . .

Such shadows as they must
cast, sharp-edged;
the whole floor, said to be crystal,
barry with them. And long!

Spokes that reach even to us,
Pinned as we are to the rim.

ROUSSEAU IN HIS DAY

So many nights the solitary lamp had burned;
So many nights his lone mind, slowing down
Deliberately, had questioned, as it turned
Mooning upon its drying stem, what arc
Over a lifetime day had moved him through.

Always he hoped he might deserve a Plutarch,
Not to be one posterity forgot.
Nor have we. He has left his mark: one tight
Inched-around circuit of the screw of light,
As glowing shadows track the life of roses
Over unchosen soil-crumbs. It was not
What he'd expected or the world supposes.

AFTER THE CALAMITOUS CONVOY (JULY 1942)

An island cast
its shadow across
the water. Where
they sat upon
the Arctic shore
it shadowed them.

The mainland rose
tawny before
their eyes and closed
round them in capes
the island must
have slid from, once.

Under one horn
of land not quite
naked, above
the anchorage
white masonry
massed round a square.

From there one gained
the waterfront
by, they perceived,
a wooden stair
that wound down through
workshops and godowns.

Admiringly
their eyes explored
make-do-and-mend:
arrangements that
the earth lent—stairs,
cabins on struts,

stages of raised
catwalks between
stair and railed stair,
staked angles, ramps
and landings in
the open air.

Roof of the world,
not ceiling. One
hung to it not
as flies do but
as steeplejacks
move over rungs.

Survivors off
the Russian run,
years later they
believed the one
stable terrain
that Arctic one.

DEPRAVITY: TWO SERMONS

(1) Americans: for their Bicentennial

The best, who could, went back—because they nursed
A need to find depravity less dispersed,
Less, as it seemed, diluted by crass hope.
So back went Henry James to evil Europe,
Unjust, unequal, cruel. Localized,
The universal could be realized
In words and not in words; not by the Press
Nor the theatrical Pulpit. Prefaces
Delineate the exquisite pains he took
To bottle up a bad smell in a book.
Inordinate pains! For Paris, London, Rome
Were not much less disorderly than back home;
There too, already, what he sought was traced
Upon no maps, but must be found by Taste,
A nostril lifted to the tainted gale
Of words, of words—all shop-soiled, all for sale.
Each year that he survived, things fell apart
Till H.G. Wells was 'Life', and he was 'Art'.
'Life'! Is it something else than life, to live
On the scent always of that faint, pervasive
Smell that alone explains what we've become?
What ought to be, and once was, axiom?

(2) St Paul's Revisited

> 'The change of Philomel, by the barbarous king,
> So rudely forced'.
> *[In the myth, Philomela became a nightingale, and
> Tereus, her ravisher, a hoopoe.]*

Anger, a white wing? No, a hoopoe's wing,
King Tereus, Hatred. Crested ravisher,
The motley lapwing whoops and whoops it up
Greek Street and Fleet Street till the gutters run
Their serial feature. Liquid, yellow, thick,

It pools here, fed from the Antipodes,
The Antilles . . . For the seven seas run with bile
To the Pool of London, sink where the ordure, talent
At home in this world, gathers. And it pools
Not only there but in whatever head
Recalls with rage the choir of Christ and Wren.

Horned and self-soiling, not the barbarous king
Of Thrace and the anthologies, nor a brute,
A plain quick killer, but degenerate,
The rapist lapwings sideways through our heads
And finds no exit. There's a place it might:
The A-to-Z preserves no record of it
Though Strype or any antique gazetteer
Describes it well enough, a Thames-side borough
Decayed already, called Depravity.
If we could find it now, our hoopoes might
Hop from inside our heads, and Thames run cleaner.

Anger won't do it. Ire! Its hooked bill gouges
The chicken-livers of its young. Irate,
We are depraved, and by that token. Gulls
Cry, and they skeeter on a candid wing
Down slopes of air, but not for anger's sake.
Spite, malice, arrogance and 'Fuck you, Jack',
Birds in the gables of Depravity
Twitter and cheep, but most inside my head
And can be lived with. But the hoopoe whoops
Always inside, and rancorous. Rancour! Rancour!
Oh patriotic and indignant bird!

SEEING HER LEAVE

'gardens bare and Greek'—Yvor Winters

This West! this ocean! The bare
Beaches, the stony creek
That no human affair
Has soiled . . . Yes, it is Greek,

What she saw as the plane
Lifted from San Jose.
Under the shadow of Wren
She walks her ward today;

Once more my tall young woman
Has nerved herself to abandon
This Greece for the Graeco-Roman
Peristyles of London,

Where the archaic, the heated,
Dishevelled and frantic Greek
Has been planed and bevelled, fitted
To the civic, the moralistic.

And that has been noble, I think,
In her and others. Such
Centuries, sweat, and ink
Spent to achieve that much!

Lloyds of London, some
Indemnity for our daughters!
Those who trust the dome
Of St Paul's to the waters . . .

So much of the price is missed
In the tally of toil, ink, years;
Count, neo-classicist,
The choking back of tears.   *(California)*

MANDELSTAM, ON DANTE

(1)
Russian Jew, for you
    To re-think Dante, dissolve
Into fluids that four-square slab
    Of Christendom, meant a resolve

(So it must seem) to taunt
    And tempt the unsteadied Gentile,
As it might be me, to act
    In nettled Stalin's style.

Dangerous, those corrosives
    You handle. First and last
Powder the graven image!
    'Jew' means 'iconoclast'.

Can we believe the impulse
    Consciously suicidal?
Or was the play of mind
    Lordly, the interest idle?

(2)
About the skies, you went wrong somewhere. Let
Some nearer neighbour of theirs make the corrections.
For them it was easier, them the nine Olympic
Dantescan discuses, to clang directions!

You are not to be thought of apart from the life you lived
And what Life intends is at once to kill and caress
That thus the distress which beat in on your ears, on your eyes
And the sockets of your eyes, be Florentine.

Let us not then assign to you, no, let us not fit about your
Hollowed-out temples that bittersweet prickle, the laurel—
Better in your case if we should split your
Heart into blue and clamorous bits of ocean.

For when you died, having served out your time,
You in your time friend to all lifetime-livers,
Yes, there transpired a broader, a loftier chime
Sent from the skies in your entire chest's heavings.

(3) *(Voronezh, 1937)*
'About the skies, I went wrong somewhere. Let
Some nearer neighbour of theirs make the corrections.
For you it was easier, you the nine Olympic

Dantescan discuses, to clang directions,
Be out of breath, get black and blue contusions . . .

But Thou, if Thou art not the heretofore's
Nothing-accomplishing hero, if Thou art bent
Standing over me now, wine-steward, to proffer the cup,
Pour me the strong wine, not the ephemeral ferment
To drink of, to pledge the vertiginous, towering, straight-up
Insane blue-azure's hand-to-hand engagement.

Dovecotes, black holes, starlings' nesting-boxes,
Blue of the bluest, case of the key at its keenest,
Ice of the heretofore, high ice!—ice of the Spring . . .
Clouds, look—the clouds, against soft collusions embattled . . .
Quiet now! Storm-clouds, see where they lead them out,
                                        bridled.'

(4)
Rhyme, you once said, only
    Points it up, tags it, the blue
Cabinet-making of Heaven
    And Earth, the elegant joints
All of them flush as given!

Symmetries in this blue
    Cabinet, the small
Rooms of stanzas—in this
    No woe, you said, but the happy
Chances of mathematics.

Clouds come and go like a French
    Polisher's breath on walnut,
Protean, fluid . . . And you
    A lordly squandering playboy!
No bequest but you blue it!

At home in the Empyrean . . .
    Yes, but one joint had sprung
Long, long ago. The woe
    Came, and was Florentine?
As well say: Galilean.

DEATH OF A PAINTER
in memoriam William Partridge

Behind the grid, the radiant
planes and translucent ledges
of colour,

the constructions,

feelingful but extreme
distortions, as my eye found them,

three or four trees and a Norman
church-tower in Leicestershire? Well
yes, if you say so.
You painted always from nature.
That mattered, you always said.

Hard to see why, unless

among these cobalts and
pale yellows, these
increments and crumblings,

in that or another churchyard
we are permitted to speak
to a Divine Distorter
these lines that you occasion.

PORTLAND
after Pasternak

Portland, the Isle of Portland—how I love
Not the place, its name! It is as if
These names were your name, and the cliff, the breaking
Of waves along a reach of tumbled stone
Were a configuration of your own
Firm slopes and curves—your clavicles, your shoulder.
A glimpse of that can set the hallway shaking.

And I am a night sky that is tired of shining,
Tired of its own hard brilliance, and I sink.

Tomorrow morning, grateful, I shall seem
 Keen, but be less clear-headed than I think;
 A brightness more than clarity will sail
Off lips that vapour formulations, make
Clear sound, full rhyme, and rational order take
Account of a dream, a sighing cry, a moan.

Like foam on all three sides at midnight lighting
Up, far off, a seaward jut of stone.

ORPHEUS

named them
and they danced,
they danced: the rocks, stones, trees.

What had possessed them,
or him? How did it help?

What had got into those stones,
throwing up puffs
of yellow dust as they bounced, and could he
hear them, an irregular percussion
there in the blinding sunlight
like a discotheque at a distance?

No, I'm afraid not: weightless.
For them to dance
they had to be light as air,
as the puff of air that named them.

Thistledown rocks! Who needs them?

Well but, they danced for joy,
his holy joy

in stones, in there being stones
there, that stones should be,
and boulders too, and trees . . .

Is that how it was? One hopes so.

ARS POETICA
in memoriam
Michael Ayrton,
sculptor

Walk quietly around in
A space cleared for the purpose.

Most poems, or the best,
Describe their own birth, and this
Is what they are—a space
Cleared to walk around in.

Their various symmetries are
Guarantees that the space has
Boundaries, and beyond them
The turbulence it was cleared from.

Small clearances, small poems;
Unlikely now the enormous
Louring, resonant spaces
Carved out by a Virgil.

The old man likes to sit
Here, in his black-tiled *loggia*
A patch of sun, and to muse
On Pasternak, Michael Ayrton.

Ayrton, he remembers,
Soon after reading his
Obituary, behold!
A vision of him:

The bearded, heavy-shouldered
London clubman, smiling
Against a *quattrocento*
View of the upper Arno.

This was in answer to prayer:
A pledge, a sufficient solace.
Poor rhyme, and are you there?
Bless Michael with your promise.

The old man likes to look
Out on his tiny *cortile*,
A flask of 'Yosemite Road'
Cheap Chablis at his elbow.   *(California)*

IN THE STOPPING TRAIN

*

I have got into the slow train
again. I made the mistake
knowing what I was doing,
knowing who had to be punished.

I know who has to be punished:
the man going mad inside me;
whether I am fleeing
from him or towards him.

This journey will punish the bastard:
he'll have his flowering gardens
to stare at through the hot window;
words like 'laurel' won't help.

He abhors his fellows,
especially children; let there
not for pity's sake
be a crying child in the carriage.

So much for pity's sake.
The rest for the sake of justice:
torment him with his hatreds
and love of fictions.

The punishing slow pace
punishes also places along the line
for having, some of them, Norman
or Hanoverian stone-work:

his old familiars, his
exclusive prophylactics.
He'll stare his fill at their
emptiness on this journey.

Jonquil is a sweet word.
Is it a flowering bush?
Let him helplessly wonder
for hours if perhaps he's seen it.

Has it a white and yellow
flower, the jonquil? Has it
a perfume? Oh his art could
always pretend it had.

He never needed to see,
not with his art to help him.
He never needed to use his
nose, except for language.

Torment him with his hatreds,
torment him with his false
loves. Torment him with time
that has disclosed their falsehood.

Time, the exquisite torment!
His future is a slow
and stopping train through places
whose names used to have virtue.

A stopping train, I thought,
was a train that was going to stop.
Why board it then, in the first place?

Oh no, they explained, it is stopping
and starting, stopping and starting.

How could it, they reasoned gently,
be always stopping unless˙
also it was always starting?

I saw the logic of that;
grown-ups were good at explaining.

Going to stop was the same
as stopping to go. What madness!
It made a sort of sense, though.

It's not, I explained, that I mind
getting to the end of the line.
Expresses have to do that.

No, they said. We see . . .
But do you? I said. It's not
the last stop that is bad . . .

No, they said, it's the last
start, the little one; yes,
the one that doesn't last.

Well, they said, you'll learn
all about that when you're older.

Of course they learned it first.
Oh naturally, yes.

*

The man in the stopping train
sees them along the highway

with a recklessness like breeding
passing and re-passing:
dormobile, Vauxhall, Volvo.

He is shrieking silently: 'Rabbits!'
He abhors his fellows.
Yet even the meagre arts
of television can
restore them to him sometimes,

when the man in uniform faces
the unrelenting camera
with a bewildered fierceness
beside the burnt-out Simca.

*

What's all this about flowers?
They have an importance he can't
explain, or else their names have.

Spring, he says, 'stirs'. It is what
he has learned to say, he can say
nothing but what he has learned.

And Spring, he knows, means flowers.
Already he observes this.
Some people claim to love them.

Love *them*? Love flowers? Love,
love . . . the word is hopeless:
gratitude, maybe, pity . . .

Pitiful, the flowers.
He turns that around in his head:
what on earth can it mean?

Flowers, it seems, are important.
And he can name them all,
identify hardly any.

*

Judith Wright, Australian

'. . . has become', I said, 'the voice
of her unhappy nation.'
O wistfully I said it.

Unhappier than it knows,
her nation. And though she will tell it,
it cannot understand:

with its terrible future before it,
glaring at its terrible past;

its disequilibrium, its
cancers in bud and growing;

all its enormous sadness
still taking off, still arcing

over the unhistoried
Pacific, humming to Chile.

Stone heads of Easter Island!
Spoiled archipelagos!

How they have suffered already
on Australia's account

and England's. They will suffer
no more on England's.

Judith Wright, Australian,
'has become', I said,

'the voice of her unhappy,
still-to-be-guilty nation.'

Wistfully I said it,
there in the stopping train.

*

The things he has been spared . . .
'Gross egotist!' Why don't
his wife, his daughter, shrill
that in his face?

Love and pity seem
the likeliest explanations;
another occurs to him—
despair too would be quiet.

*

Time and again he gave battle,
furious, mostly effective;
nobody counts the wear
and tear of rebuttal.

Time and again he rose
to the flagrantly offered occasion;
nobody's hanged for a slow
murder by provocation.

Time and again he applauded
the stand he had taken; how much
it mattered, or to what
assize, is not recorded.

Time and again he hardened
his heart and his perceptions;
nobody knows just how
truths turn into deceptions.

Time and again, oh time and
that stopping train!
Who knows when it comes to a stand,
and will not start again?

* (Son et Lumière)
I have travelled with him many times
now. Already we nod,
we are almost on speaking terms.

Once I thought that he sketched
an apologetic gesture
at what we turned away from.

Apologies won't help him:
his spectacles flared like paired
lamps as he turned his head.

I knew they had been ranging,
paired eyes like mine,
igniting and occluding

coppice and crisp chateau,
thatched corner, spray of leaf,
curved street, a swell of furrows,

where still the irrelevant vales
were flowering, and the still
silver rivers slid west.

*

The dance of words
is a circling prison, thought
the passenger staring through
the hot unmoving pane
of boredom. It is not
thank God a dancing pain,
he thought, though it starts to jig
now. (The train is moving.) 'This',
he thought in rising panic
(Sit down! Sit down!)
'this much I can command,
exclude. Dulled words, keep still!
Be the inadequate, cloddish
despair of me!' No good:
they danced, as the smiling land
fled past the pane, the pun's
galvanized *tarantelle*.

*

'A shared humanity . . .' He
pummels his temples. 'Surely,
surely that means something

He knew too few in love,
too few in love.

That sort of foolish beard
masks an uncertain mouth.
And so it proved: he took
some weird girl off to a weird
commune, clutching at youth.

Dear reader, this is not
our chap, but another.
Catch our clean-shaven hero
tied up in such a knot?
A cause of so much bother?

He knew too few in love.

HIS THEMES
(after reading Edmond Jabès)

His themes? Ah yes he had themes.
It was what we all liked about him.
Especially I liked it.
One knew, nearly always one knew
what he was talking about, and he talked
in such a ringing voice.

What did he talk about? What,
just what were his themes?
Oh, of the most important!

Loss was one of his themes;
he told us, as any bard should,
    the story of our people
    (tribe), he had memorized
    chronologies, genealogies,
    the names and deeds of heroes,
    the succession of our kings,
    our priests, the sept of our pipers,
    the mediations . . . and this
    while, young and old,
    we extolled the immediate, meaning
    the unremembering. *Yes,*
    and what was his theme? His theme, you said, was . . .?
Loss. Loss was his theme.

And duty. He taught us our duty;
he taught us, as any
legislator should,
    the rules of hygiene, the clean
    and the unclean meats, the times and
    the means of fumigation,
    the strewing and spreading, of fires,
    and what to do with the old
    and how to dispose of the dead
    and how to live with our losses
    uncomplaining . . . and this
    while, young and old,
    we did our best to be free,
    meaning unruly. *Yes,*
    and what was his theme? What did you say his theme was?

Duty. His theme was duty.

Fear also. Fear was a theme;
he taught us, as all seers must,
continual apprehension:
    of one another, of
    our womenfolk and our
    male children, of
    the next clan over the mountains

and of the mountains, also
the waters, the heavenly bodies
wheeling and colliding,
of the wild beasts both large
and infinitesimal, of
revenants and of the future,
and of the structure of matter
and of the unknown . . . and all this
while, young and old,
we tried to keep our nerve,
meaning, to be heedless. *Yes,
and what was the theme, did you say, of this voice both
hollow and ringing?*

Fear. Fear was the theme.

We like to be told these things.
We need to be reminded.

*He sounds like a sort of priest.
What was your priesthood doing?*

Nonsensical things, like spinning
a shallow great bowl of words
poised on the stick of a question,
pointing it this way and that
for an answering flash, as the bend
of a river may come in a flash
over miles and miles
from a fold in the hills, over miles.

We paid them no attention.

TO THOM GUNN IN LOS ALTOS, CALIFORNIA

Conquistador! Live dangerously, my Byron,
In this metropolis
Of Finistère. Drop off
The edge repeatedly, and come

Back to tell us! Dogs and cherry-trees
Are not your element, although
You like them well enough when, cast
Ashore and briefly beached, our Commodore,
You take a turn among them, your cigar
Fragrant along a sunny garden wall,
Home between voyages, with your aunts in Kent.

Home . . . Is that home? Is even Land's End 'home'?
You shrug and say we are mid-Atlantic people,
You and I. I'd say for you
The mid-Pacific rather: somewhere out
On the International Dateline, so far out
Midsummer Oregon and midwinter Chile
Are equidistant, and 'the slow
Pacific swell' you generate lifts and crunches
Under the opalescent high fog with as much
Patience in one hemisphere as the other,
An exhalation from the depths you sound to.

The plesiosaur! Your lead-line has gone down to
The Age of Reptiles, even as
Over your head the flying lizard
Sprung from its Lompoc silo, Vandenberg Airforce Base,
Tracks high across mid-ocean to its target.
Ignore it, though a tidal wave will rage
From where it plunges, flood Japan
And poison Asia. This is the pacific
Ocean, the peacemaker. Nothing rhymes with this
Lethal indifference that you plumbed to even
Once in a bath-house in Sonoma County.

This is the end of the world. At the end, at the edge
We live among those for whom
As is natural enough
The edge is the navel of earth, and the end, the beginning.
Hope springs not eternal nor everywhere—does it
Spring in Kent? For these our friends, however,
It springs, it springs. Have we a share in it?
This is the Garden of Eden, the serpent coiled

Inside it is sleepy, reposeful. It need not flex
A muscle to take us. What are we doing here?
What am I doing, I who am scared of edges?

SEUR, NEAR BLOIS

That a toss of wheat-ears lapping
Church-walls should placate us
Is easy to understand
In the abstract. That in fact
The instance of seeing also
A well with its wrought-iron stanchion,
Of feeling a balmy coolness,
Of hearing a Sunday noon silence,
Of smelling the six ragged lime-trees,
A church-door avenue, should
Placate, compose, is as much
As to say that the eye and the nose,
Also the ear and the very
Surface of one's skin is
An ethical organ; and further,
If indeed it is further
Or even other, a learned
Historian of man's culture.

GEMONA-DEL-FRIULI, 1961-1976

We have written to Giulia, saying
'Are you still alive?'
And no reply comes.
This is a bad look out.

What sort of a life this is
I thought I knew, or I learned,
Some 15 years ago
Precisely in Giulia's country:

Gemona, the heartland, the forests
Living in an orange light
After calamity. That one!
That was the place;

Where a calamity, not
In any case undeserved,
Chastened, I thought, and instructed
Gravely, biddable me

As to the proper proportions
Of the dead to the living, of death
To life, and out of all
Proportion, love . . . Now this!

Earthquake! And the entire
Small city of Gemona
Flat in one enormous
Stir of that rock-ribbed earth

Which had not in 700
Years—for some of Gemona
Had stood that long—not stirred
Like that in 700 years.

What colour of justification,
What nice, austere proportion
Now can be put on the mountains?
At whose hand this chastisement?

AN APPARITION

Gina, I saw you walk
Suddenly, in white
Brassiere and panties under
A fish-net wrap; your sallow skin,

Firm and sullen to fire,
Inflamed the Panamanian

Day to exceptional ardours
In Tehuantepec Bay

As our Edwardian prow
Ploughed southward, and decrepit
Bodies basked in renewed
Delusory bronze and vigour.

The posh ships, P. & O.,
Trace in phosphorescent
Peppermint-fire on the oceans
An after-image of Empire.

The sun stooped down to take you,
Stiff on your bed in Boulder,
Colorado, Gina;
You will never grow older,

Nor will your empire ever,
Italo-American girl,
Crumble in Eritrea,
Dear wraith, raped by Apollo.

HORAE CANONICAE

PRIME

New every morning is the love
Our wakening and uprising prove,
Bond it in warranty a hundred proof.
Giving his thanks for roof, for bed and board,
Mr Saint Keble, meek and lowly,
White with rite, and clean with holy,
Wordplays to the morning's Lord.

TERCE

New every morning is the power
That activates us, active though we are . . .
At 9 o'clock, the scriptural 3rd hour,

Mr Saint William Law is eating his
Sweet humble pie: 'We have no more
Power of our own to move a hand or stir
A foot, than to stop clouds, or move the sun.'

SEXT
'Filling us with such bowels of
Compassion as when' (Come, Mr Law, we are furnished
With bowels, and they are full, or they are not;
What room for other organs?), glimpsing her
Appallingly in Cambridge Circus, tracing
The faceless angel who mounted her once and vanished,
'We see the miseries of an hospital.'

NONES
At 3 o'clock in the afternoon,
Loggy with gin, with wine, with Mexican beer,
Resignation to the will of God
Comes easy. That it should be 'hardly worth
Living in a world so full of changes
And revolutions'—ah, how wrong! Yet dozing,
Fanned in a garden-chair, is hardly 'prayer'.

VESPERS
This one for the telling of sins. And for
The original horror, the victimization, no problem.
But for our own, our particular own, in the sorry
Unrollings, where was the harm? Not nowhere, but
Where? In prayer, no place for 'all-over-the-place',
It comes to seem . . . My instructors' awful calm
Tell-tales the stink: half spunk, half frightened sweat.

COMPLINE
Now I lay me down to sleep
Perhaps not to wake, and I am alone in the house!
How much alone in whatever house of bone,
Suddenly I love my fellow creatures
So much, though for that the hour was Sext, was noon.
I tell you over feverishly, my loved ones.
You are my own, you are? My own! My own?

MORNING

Rose late: the jarring and whining
Of the parked cars under my windows, their batteries drained,
Somehow was spared. When I let out our schoolboy
Into the street, it was light: the place was alive and scented.

Spared too, for the most part, the puzzling tremulousness
That afflicts me often, these mornings. (I think
Either I need, so early, the day's first drink or
This is what a sense of sin amounts to:
Aghast incredulity at the continued success
Of an impersonation, the front put on to the world,
The responsibilities . . .)
                              Let all that go:
Better things throng these nondescript, barged-through streets
(The sun! The February sun, so happily far and hazy . . .)
Than a mill of ideas.
                        Sin, I will say, comes awake
With all the other energies, even at last the spark
Leaps on the sluggard battery, and one should have
Prosopopoeia everywhere: Stout Labour
Gets up with his pipe in his mouth or lighting
The day's first *Gauloise-filtre*; then stout
Caffein like a fierce masseur
Rams him abreast of the day; stout Sin
Is properly a-tremble; stout
Vociferous Electricity chokes and chokes,
Stumbles at last into coughings, and will soon
Come to the door with a telegram—'Operation
Some Day This Week'; and stout
Love gets up out of rumpled sheets and goes singing
Under his breath to the supermarket, the classroom,
The briskly unhooded
Bureaucratic typewriter. See how
Sol winks upon its clever keys, and Flora
In a northern winter, far underground,
Feels herself sore at nubs and nipples.

And that mob of ideas? Don't knock them. The sick pell-mell
Goes by the handsome Olympian name of Reason.

TO A TEACHER OF FRENCH

Sir, you were a credit to whatever
Ungrateful slate-blue skies west of the Severn
Hounded you out to us. With white, cropped head,
Small and composed, and clean as a Descartes
From as it might be Dowlais, 'Fiery' Evans
We knew you as. You drilled and tightly lipped
Le futur parfait dans le passé like
The Welsh Guards in St James's, your pretence
Of smouldering rage an able sergeant-major's.

We jumped to it all right whenever each
Taut smiling question fixed us. Then it came:
Crash! The ferrule smashed down on the first
Desk of the file. You whispered: *Quelle bêtise!*
Ecoutez, s'il vous plait, de quelle bêtise
On est capable!
                Yet you never spoke
To us of poetry; it was purely language,
The lovely logic of its tenses and
Its accidence that, mutilated, moved you
To rage or outrage that I think was not
At all times simulated. It would never
Do in our days, dominie, to lose
Or seem to lose your temper. And besides
Grammarians are a dying kind, the day
Of histrionic pedagogy's over.

You never taught me Ronsard, no one did,
But you gave me his language. He addressed
The man who taught him Greek as *Toi qui dores*
(His name was Jean Dorat) *la France de l'or.*
I couldn't turn a phrase like that on 'Evans';
And yet you gild or burnish something as,
At fifty in the humidity of Touraine,
Time and again I profit by your angers.

WIDOWERS

'i segni dell' antica fiamma'

Atheist, Laodicean or
Whatever name our hand-to-mouth evasions
Earn for us, all of us have the thought
That states of soul in some uncertain sort
Survive us—sealed, it could be, in locations:
A yard, a coomb, an inn, a Cornish tor.

These leak their fragrances. To tap the fount
Of consolation calls on us for no
Dexterity at first; it isn't hard
To bruise a hip by falling in that yard
Or on that hillside. Hurt is all we know,
Stout alpenstock as we begin to mount

The purgatorial steeps, the terraces
Kicked back behind us. Then we sweat, we stink,
We fear that we forget. Our ancient haunts
Glow far above us, and the glimmer taunts
Our coming numbness. There she dwells, we think . . .
She does, although our need to think so passes.

SOME SHIRES REVISITED

(1) NORFOLK

The scroll is defaced; the worm
Is in the roof; and the flaking
Inscription may be cleared
Of ivy but, if it is read,
It must be on the firm
Presumption it is mistaken.

Reading from haunted air
Certain great (which is not to say, good)
Historical presences—Walpole,
Nelson, landmarks in Norfolk—

I had readers who thought that I could
Never in fact have been there.

(2) DEVONSHIRE ·

'Into Spooner's, looking for remnants,'
Said Mrs John; and her face was wistful
As if the town she recalled, the tenements
Burnt in the blitz, the streets like tunnels
Turning and twisting at cliff-like corners
Under the web of the wires, were a haven
Unspeakably lovely and calm. The destroyers
Had threatened her future; the young rebuilders
Tore down that future perfect in the past
Of a new-planned Plymouth, 1951.

(3) LEICESTERSHIRE

Clinton-Baddeley, Richards,
Blunden . . . these I have blessed:
Three good men named, and as many
Of those who invited them there
Unnamed, their equals or betters,
Upholders of what they professed
To care for, the world of letters
In the not quite wholly benighted
Midlands of England. In these
Worthies I have delighted
With a droll rhyme or two;
Leicestershire, when it housed them,
Did better than it knew.

(4) STAFFORDSHIRE
for Charles Tomlinson

'As once on Thracian Hebrus side' (to use
Your own Etrurian idiom, jasper-ware)

   'The tree-enchanter Orpheus fell
   By Bacchanalians torn',

So I have seen you—gasping, bloodied—fall
Time and again over twenty-five years, and the Maenads

Quite honestly astonished: 'But we surely
(Serenely, suavely) always gave him his due?'

Your love of our country has not been returned, and won't be.

(5) BEDFORDSHIRE

Crop-headed nonconformists,
    Cromwell's Ironsides, sprang
Out of this clay. But not all
    The sour battalions rang
With benedictions when
    The sage dictator willed
    A king was to be killed.

Redbrick, round-windowed chapels,
    Squat on these gravels, rose,
And yet not all their broadcloth,
    When the time came, chose
The Red Flag as the only
    Colours to march to. Some
    Never came back from the Somme.

Born one of them, I think
    How it might be to be French;
How Protestants might man
    Pétain's untenable trench
And, rendering unto Caesar
    What's due to Caesar, might
    Die fighting the wrong good fight.

GRUDGING RESPECT

As when a ruined face
Lifted among those crowding
For the young squire's largesse
Perceives him recognize
Her and she grabs, not for any
Languidly lofted penny
They scrabble for, but for his eyes
And pockets them, their clouding
That instant; and the abruptness
With which his obliging is checked,
His suddenly leaving the place . . .

Just so may a grudging respect
Be, from a despised one,
Not just better than none
At all, but sweeter than any.

A SPRING SONG

'stooped to truth and moralized his song'

Spring pricks a little. I get out the maps.
Time to demoralize my song, high time.
Vernal a little. *Primavera*. First
Green, first truth and last.
High time, high time.

A high old time we had of it last summer?
I overstate. But getting out the maps . . .
Look! Up the valley of the Brenne,
Louise de la Vallière . . . Syntax collapses.
High time for that, high time.

To Château-Renault, the tannery town whose marquis
Rooke and James Butler whipped in Vigo Bay
Or so the song says, an amoral song
Like Ronsard's where we go today
Perhaps, perhaps tomorrow.

Tomorrow and tomorrow and . . . Get well!
Philip's black-sailed familiar, avaunt
Or some word as ridiculous, the whole
Diction kit begins to fall apart.
High time it did, high time.

High time and a long time yet, my love!
Get out that blessed map.
Ageing, you take your glasses off to read it.
Stooping to truth, we potter to Montoire.
High time, my love. High time and a long time yet.

TOWNEND, 1976

When does a town become a city? This
That ends where I begin it, at Townend
With Wright the Chemist (one of the few not changed),
Grows cityfied, though still my drab old friend.

Thanks therefore for the practical piety
Of E. G. Tasker, antiquarian;
His *Barnsley Streets*. Unshed, my tears hang heavy
Upon the high-gloss pages where I scan

What else, though, but remembered homely squalor?
Generations of it! Eldon Street
Smells of bad drains of forty years ago
Ah sweetly. But should penury smell sweet?

An end to it then. An end to that town. Townend.
A Tetley's house, the Wheatsheaf, holds its station
Since 1853, where Dodworth Road
Stars into five streets, 'major intersection'.

Portentous words! Hoist up to suit South Yorkshire's
Administrative centre, such perforce
This town must live with, must live up or down to:
'Intersection'; 'shopping precinct'; 'concourse' . . .

And not to be sneered nor sniffed at. This is not,
It never was, Blackheath or Tunbridge Wells;
No buildings 'listed', nor deserving it,
Press to be saved as civic ardour swells.

Of cities much is written. Even Scripture
Has much to say of them, though mostly under
The inauspicious name of 'Babylon'.
What a town is, one is left to wonder.

Is homely squalor, then, its sign and function?
Is it a swollen village? If it is,
Are swellings lanced? Have towns a size or shape
More than villages and less than cities?

I think of the Irish, or perhaps the Celtic
'Townland'. (Also, 'township' might provoke us.)
'Townland', so my Irish years persuade me,
Means never a star of roads, never a focus.

Never! By no means! There's a lead at last:
Focus, a hearth. The English circumstance
In town or village draws to a hearth, a fug:
Townend, the up-draught up five flues at once!

Whatever meets that need, it's certain 'concourse',
'Complex' nor 'intersection' ever could.
Upon their hunkers, 'carring' (cowering) down
By a spent flame, the colliers of my boyhood . . .

That was in the 'thirties, 'the Depression';
Outside whatever pub it is in Kingstone,
Unwanted in the open, nipping air,
All the one class, a hardship town, all one.

Something, I take it, not to be found in cities;
No, nor in villages, what with parson, squire,
Farmer and farm-hand. (Just as well: the once
And ever martyred stoke a sullen fire.)

Up above Glossop, weeping cloud at Woodhead;
Up again after, over the last high hogsback,
The clean black waters shine up steel, not silver,
The peat is black, the lowering skies are black.

Millicent Dillon, if you ever visit
This town as you say you will, this is the way:
Ashbourne to Buxton, Buxton to Glossop, over
To an ash-boled England and a Baltic day.

For this is under us now, as we come down:
The Silkstone seam, where woods compacted lay
Shade upon shade, multiplication of blackness
That seeps up through: '*black* Barnsley', we would say.

The sneer of it—black Barnsley, that my mother
Indignantly thought corrupted out of 'bleak',
'Bleak Barnsley'. Who else cared? Corruption in
All that we do, decay in all we speak.

Ireland, America, the Atlantic writ
Here runs no longer. Out of the sunset shires,
Ireland, and Wales, they called us; and we shut
Behind us the West that beckons, that aspires.

Westward, the moors: shield more than barrier, closing
Utopias off. We were not to be tricked:
Depravity stalked the streets with us. A city
Needs, on the contrary, a red-light district.

Barracks, industrial barracks: 'town'
In that late sense. Sensational the feat,
Making a city of the regimental
Lines, as you might say: Day Street, Peel Street, Pitt Street!

Well, it has started; air is let in, and light,
All to the good. And now what will befall?
Concourse and complex, underpass and precinct,
The scale not human but angelical:

Squalor on that scale; homeliness as 'home'
Might be for Rebel Angels, or their hordes,
Machinists of 'machines for living in';
No fug upon the windy drawing-boards!

Some things get better: not *in situ*, in
Stone (that gets worse), or steel; but in
Our knowing, though our architect were Wren,
We live in Babylon, we aspire in sin.

The end of a town—however mean, however
Much of a byword—marks the end of an age,
An age of worn humility. Hereafter,
The Prince of Darkness and his equipage!

THREE FOR WATER-MUSIC (1981)

THE FOUNTAIN OF CYANË

I.

Her father's brother rapes her!
               In the bright
Ovidian colours all is for delight,
The inadmissible minglings are recounted
With such finesse: the beery ram that mounted
His niece and, hissing 'Belt up', had her, is
Hell's grizzly monarch gaunt in tapestries;
The thrashing pallid skivvy under him
A vegetation myth; the stinking slum
Is Enna's field where Phoebus ne'er invades
The tufted fences, nor offends the shades;
And her guffawing Ma assumes the land,
Coarsely divine, cacophonous, gin in hand.
Sky-blue, dark-blue, sea-green, cerulean dyes
Dye into fables what we hoped were lies
And feared were truths. A happy turn, a word,
Says they are both, and nothing untoward.
Coloured by rhetoric, to die of grief
Becomes as graceful as a falling leaf;
No chokings, retchings, not the same as dying
Starved and worn out because you can't stop crying.
Cyanë's fable, that one; how she wept
Herself away, shocked for her girl-friend raped—
'Her varied members to a fluid melt,
A pliant softness in her bones is felt . . .'
Sweet lapse, sweet lapse . . . 'till only now remains
Within the channel of her purple veins
A silver liquor . . .' Ah, the master's touch
So suave, mere word-play, that can do so much!
And now at last imperious, in bad taste:
'Nothing to fill love's grasp; her husband chaste
Bathes in that bosom he before embrac'd.'
The spring-fed pool that is Cyanë may
Be visited in Sicily today;
And what's to be made of that? Or how excuse
Our intent loitering outside Syracuse?

II.

Modesty, I kept saying,
Temperate, temperate . . . Yes,
The papyrus were swaying
Hardly at all, and late,
Late in the season the rings
Widened upon the reedy
Pool, and the beady-eyed frogs
Volleyed out after mayfly.

Fountain? No jet, no spume,
Spew nor spurt . ; . Was this
Where Pluto's chariot hurtled
Up out of 'gloomy Dis'?
Male contumely for that
First most seminal rape,
Proserpine's, prescribes
Some more vertiginous landscape.

Late, late in that season . . .
Easy, easy the lap
And rustle of blue waters . . .
Wholly a female occasion
This, as Demeter launches
One fish in a silver arc
To signalize her daughter's
Re-entry to the dark.

III.

The balked, the aborted vision
Permits of the greater finesse;
The achieved one is fugitive, slighter,
One might almost say, 'loose'.

And yet the oceanic
Swells of an unencumbered
Metric jiggle the planes
Epiphanies must glow from.

So, though one might almost say 'loose',
One mustn't. They like the closed-off

Precincts all right, but never
When those exult in their closures.

The shrine is enclosed from the bare
Fields and, three miles away
Clearly in sight, the high-rise
Shimmering haze of the city.

But the fence is of wire; the warped
Palings give easy access;
No turnstile; and at the pool
Of Cyanë, nothing to pay;

No veil to be rent, no grille,
No holy of holies. The Greek
World, one is made to remember,
Was Christianized quite early.

Epiphanies all around us
Always perhaps. And some
Who missed the flash of a fin
Were keeping their eyes on rhyme-schemes.

   IV.
And so with stanzas . . . moving
From room to room is a habit adapted to winter,
Warm and warming, worship Sunday by Sunday,
And one is glad of it. But when
Now and again I turn the knob and enter
The special chill where my precarious Springs
Hang water-beaded in still air, I hear
A voice announce: 'And this is the
Conservatory!' Greenish misted panes
Of mystifying memory conserve
In an unnatural silence nymph and pool;
It is an outside room, at the end of a range of rooms
But still a room, accounted for or even
Entered upon the impatient plans in my
Infidel youth. At that time no
Nymph, and no pool: still, it appears,
Room left for them—and yet

Rooms should have an outside door, I think;
I wilt for lack of it, though my plants do not.

V.
     Yet there was enough in this—
And it was nothing, nothing at all
     'Happened'—enough in this
     Non-happening to cap
     What Scripture says of the Fall

     Which, though it equally may
Not in that sense have happened, is
     A postulate day by day
     Called for, to explain
     Our joys, our miseries.

     A fish jumped, silver; small
Frogs took the mayfly; papyrus
     In the Sicilian fall
     Of the leaf was bowing. How
     That weightless weighed with us!

     Why, when an unheard air
Stirred in the fronds, did we assume
     An occidental care
     For proximate cause? Egyptian
     Stems abased their plume.

     So inattentive we are
We think ourselves unfallen. This
     Pool, when Pluto's car
     Whirled up, was wept by Cyanë
     For her abducted mistress.

     One could go round and round
This single and Sicilian less
     Than happening, and ground
     Therein what might suffuse
     Our lives with happiness.

I.

A poet's lie!
        The boarhound and the boar
Do not pursue their pattern as before.
What English eyes since Dryden's thought to scan
Our spinneys for the Presbyterian,
The tusked, the native beast inflamed to find
And rend the spotted or the milk-white hind,
The true Church, or the half-true? Long ago
Where once were tusks, neat fangs began to grow;
Citizen of the World and Friend to Man,
The presbyter's humanitarian.
The poor pig learned to flute: the brute was moved
By plaudits of a conscience self-approved;
'Self in benevolence absorb'd and lost'
Absorbed a ruinous Redemption's cost.

This too a lie; a newer zealot's, worse
Than any poet's in or out of verse.
These were the hunting-calls, and this the hound,
Harried the last brave pig from English ground;
Now ermine, whited weasel, sinks his tooth
Deeper than wolf or boar into the Truth.
Extinct, the English boar; he leaves a lack.
Hearts of the disinherited grow black.

II.

When he grew up
in the England of silver
cigarette cases and
Baptist chapel on Sundays,

long white flannels were still
worn, and the Mission Fields
ripe for the scything Gospel
cost him a weekly penny.

The missionary box!
It rattled as he knocked it,

crouching nearer the wireless:
deuce, Fred Perry serving . . .

Doggedly he applies
himself to the exhumations:
these pre-war amateurs,
that missionary martyr.

As gone as Cincinnatus!
Still tongue-in-cheek revered, as
Republican virtue by
a silver-tongued florid Empire,

tired of that even, lately.

 III.
To Loughwood Meeting House,
Redeemed since and re-faced,
Once persecuted Baptists
Came across sixty miles
Of Devon. Now we ask
Our own good wincing taste
To show the way to Heaven.

But if under clear-glassed windows,
The clear day looking in,
We should be always at worship
And trusting in His merits
Who saves us from the pathos
Of history, and our fears
Of natural disasters,

What antiquarian ferrets
We have been! As idle
An excrescence as Ionic
Pilasters would be, or
Surely the Puritan poet:
Burning, redundant candle,
Invisible at noon.

We are, in our way, at worship;
Though in the long-deflowered

Dissenting chapel that
England is, the slim
Flame of imagination,
Asymmetrical, wavers,
Starving for dim rose-windows.

   IV.
And so he raged exceedingly,
excessively indeed, he raged excessively
and is said to have been drunk, as certainly
in some sense and as usual he was;
lacking as usual, and in some
exorbitant measure, charity,
candour in an old sense. How
a black heart learns white-heartedness, you tell me!

Raged, and beshrewed his audience of one
without much or at all
intending it, having his eyes not on
her but on the thing to be hunted down;
or so he will excuse himself, without
much confidence. The rapist's plea:
not her but womankind. He has
the oddest wish for some way to disgrace himself.

How else can a pharisee clear the accounts, and live?

   V.
Wild Boar Clough . . . known to his later boyhood
    As the last gruelling stage before,
Feet and collar-bones raw, the tarmacadam
    Past unbelievable spa-hotels
Burned to the train at Buxton. Julian Symons,
    His poems, *Confessions of X*, reviewed
In *Poetry London*, bought on Buxton Station . . .

A nut-brown maid whom he cannot remember
    Sold him herb beer, a farmhouse brew,
One day above Wild Boar Clough, whose peat-sieved brown
    Waters were flecked below them. Legs

Were strong then, heart was light, was white, his swart
    Limbs where the old glad Adam in him,
Lissom and slim, exulted, carried him.

Somewhere that boy still swings to the trudging rhythm,
    In some brown pool that girl still reaches
A lazy arm. The harm that history does us
    Is grievous but not final. As
The wild boar still in our imaginations
    Snouts in the bracken, outward is
One steep direction gleefully always open.

So Lud's Church hides in Cheshire thereabouts
    Cleft in the moor. The slaughtered saints
Cut down of a Sunday morning by dragoons
    Grounded the English Covenant
In ling and peat-moss. Sound of singing drifts
    Tossed up like spume, persistently
Pulsing through history and out of it.

I.

A boy turned to a newt!
                        A chuffy lad
Who dared be sly when Demeter ran mad
At loss, at rapine, or to find her rule
Of nature crossed to make a girl a pool.
A filmy scarf of water . . . and that first
Apparition liquefied, dispersed.
None of us but has indulged the same
Insanity, holding Sicily to blame
For tendering first the lovely benefit
Rushed at and clasped, and then retracting it.
But loss of love has nothing to do with place.
Time ticks, a flaw flies on the water's face
But that is not it either. Remonstrate
As Arethusa may, expatriate
From Elis, threading underseas, who found
Vent for Greek waters on Sicilian ground,
It cannot help. The loves that we have lost
Are not, like her, translated or transposed,
Somewhere intact. Who ever read, for these
Poor palliatives, the *Metamorphoses*?

II.

  'Arethusa arose
    From her couch of snows
In the Akrokeraunian mountains . . .'
    More thrilling today
    My mother's way
With Shelley, than this fountain's
    Circus of grey
    Mullet, or sway
Of papyrus-fronds. Pulsations
    Still rill it through;
    What once she knew
Of crags, reverberations,
    Couches of snows,
    The nymph still knows,

Still pushing her liquid lever
        Up and out,
        As when it brought
Greeks once in a choleric fever
        To Syracuse.
        Mother, my Muse,
These are the springs that matter:
        Small thrills sustain
        The source, not vain
Glories, nor consonants' clatter
        Down a moraine
        In Shelley's brain
But smaller vaunts. One day
        In a parlour-game,
        Required to name
Mountains beginning with A,
        Proudly, aged ten,
        I pronounced it then;
The Akrokeraunian Mountains!
        Grown-ups demurred;
        But sand-grains stirred
Then, as now, in those fountains!

   III.
To have failed to
measure up
not to myth, but to
the need for gratitude . . .

In a desert of
ingratitude, this was one
small triumph, one
spout of a filial spring.

   IV.
At Syracuse the blue pool,
Dragonflies, leaping silver.
But here, at Naxos . . .
Trouble.
        In the cafés

Of Taormina the black
American sailors, and the white
Sat at separate tables, and an old
Anglo-Sicilian made
Trouble; and 'Attaboy, Yank'
Was the best I could do for
Those beardless boys,
Not themselves enamoured
Of Europe, but enacting
Their hope against its hopelessness, like any
American *inamorato*, like the type
Of all of them, the pontifical Henry James.

They had made the Naxos passage, and their old
Destroyer lay for a day and two nights offshore
In a spill of dangerous late-October light
Over the shoulder of Etna, watery, weak
And inconstant as any American's sense of Europe.
And we had been to Naxos, had descended
The gradient of millennia, and met
Trouble: the male will splayed across its Honda
Wristily revving, and the motor-coaches,
Though out of season, nosing the Holiday Inn.

So when we made it at last
To the Cyclopean wall
And the sacred mound
Sheer from the shingle where the exhausted galleys
Lay beached once, blocked
Now from the sea by a tall and later wall,
Stillness there was, a profusion of late blossoms
In the leafy place, and we were grateful, lingered
For the trouble to settle, settle. But the god
Awaited in vain indignantly the lunge
Of a silver fin in our thinned-out devotions,
The blue burn of the dragonfly, living ingot,
Flaw in the too late amber of our season.

V.

The one in the poem is not
The one that you will visit.
Syracuse you may visit,
The poem also—one
Casts no light on the other.

Through the one there strays
One and one only walker.
The city has its claim
Upon this one who can
Meet it in curious ways:

By brilliant turn of phrase?
No. For it is the past
Is brilliant, Pasternak says;
The debt we owe it, only
More modest coin repays.

So in the padlocked, man-walled
Fountain of Arethusa
Papyrus wave, but of course
Cigarette-packets float
Above Ortygia.

Not a hard lesson to learn
That this is proper, since
History has to happen;
In this case at least it seems
A not unwarranted freedom.

And so in the verdant, man-made
Latomìa, a grotto
Loud with seepage houses
No lonely inscrutable Tristan
And Iseult, but a rope-walk!

Ropemakers gone from under
Mottled impendings, still
Their hempen gossamers ran

Taut and knee-high through the shafted
Light and the cavernous air.

Gratitude, Need, and Gladness—
These are the names of the walker,
These are the strands of the hemp:
Gladness at meeting the need
The gratitude imposes.

This is our walker's scope.
You think he makes too bold?
To make this visit, think
Of how to test a rope:
Swing on it, trust it to hold.

A gimcrack drum with spikes,
Knee-high, the T-shaped stretchers . . .
This is the phrase he will use:
Warm honesties of makeshift
Transvalue Syracuse.

THE BATTERED WIFE
& OTHER POEMS (1982)

PART ONE

THE BATTERED WIFE

She thinks she was hurt this summer
More than ever before,
Beyond what there is cure for.

He has failed her once too often:
Once, it turns out, more
Than she had bargained for

In a bargain that of course
Nobody ever struck!
Oh, she had trusted her luck

Not once too often, but
All along the line:
And even this last time,

This summer, when reduced
To surely the bone her hope

Was just to live it through, his
Incalculable enmity
Rose up and struck. That he

Could no more calculate
Nor understand it than
She can, absolves the man

For the first time no longer. He
Will come back, she knows. She dreads it yet
Hopes for it, his coming back. A planet

Or else a meteor curves at the extreme
Bend of its vector, vehicle of
Prodigy and plague, and hopeless love.

G.M B.
(10.7.77)

Old oak, old timber, sunk and rooted
    In the organic cancer
Of Devon soil, the need she had
    You could not answer.

Old wash and wump, the narrow seas
    Mindlessly breaking
She scanned lifelong; and yet the tide
    There's no mistaking

She mistook. She never thought,
    It seems, that the soft thunder
She heard nearby, the pluck and slide,
    Might tow her under.

I have as much to do with the dead
    And dying, as with the living
Nowadays; and failing them is
    Past forgiving.

As soon be absolved for that, as if
    A tree, or a sea, should be shriven;
And yet the truth is, fail we must
    And be forgiven.

SHORT RUN TO CAMBORNE

The hideousness of the inland spine of Cornwall!
Redeemed (for of course in the long run all,
All is redeemed), but Wesley's chapels and all
In the slipstream of our short run rock rock to their fall.

And we surge on for Camborne, cheapness cheapened
By our going by as, with wreaths to honour the end
Of one who endured this cheapness, with our reeking
Put-put exhaust we exhaust the peace we are seeking.

Cheapness of granite-chips on the oil-starred road above Looe;
Our wanderings from the Wesleys and (it's true)
Dear-bought though they were, heaven-sent, their wanderings
                                                    too . . .
Surge, surge we may but stray is all we do.

The spinelessness of the rock-ribbed once! The riven
Granite of Wesley's gospel that all are forgiven
Since all are redeemed . . . The loose shale slides and shelves
As we forgive each other and ourselves.

All are forgiven, or may be. But we owe
This much to our dead sister (at Polperro
Pixies and trivia . . .): humanly we know
Some things are unforgivable, even so.

LIVINGSHAYES
(A tradition of Silverton, Devon)

'Live-in-ease', and then to wash
    Their sins in Lily Lake
On Corpus Christi, for their own
    And their Redeemer's sake.

Easy living, with that clear
    And running stream below;
First contract the harm, and then
    Wash it white as snow.

Not altogether. Chris Cross first,
    'The top of a high hill.'
Living it up and easy needs
    Him hung and bleeding still.

THE ADMIRAL TO HIS LADY

With you to Bideford,
Too old for stomaching
Rebuffs, not soon deterred
Nor often crossed of late,
I boomed along, not brooking
      The sky's mandate.

Habits of testy command
Forgot to say 'weather permitting'.
Though gales had rocked the land
And us, early and late,
There I was, squalls intermitting,
      Still hectoring fate.

Yet rained on, shoulders bowed,
Colour too high, too florid
In manner, voice too loud,
I felt like a youngster with you
That day, as wet winds flurried
      Torridge askew.

Wrecked body, barque of your wrecked
Hopes, or some of them—bitter
Reflections? . . . Harbours reflect
The changefulness of skies;
Bideford's waters glitter
      Like your hurt eyes.

Still, as the afterskirts
Of one black patch streel over
I brew up the next. It hurts
Each time a little less;
To cope with a demon lover
      Learn carelessness.

That rocking, jaunty way
You have, like Torridge's waters
Dancing into the bay . . .

You know what serves your turn;
You have, of all Eve's daughters,
      The least to learn!

SCREECH-OWL

I had to assure myself:
What it seemed I heard . . .
Was it my own stale self
Exhaled, or was it a bird?

Therefore with pride and relief,
Half-awake, coughing in bed,
I assure myself that screech
Came from outside my head.

Not the disgusting pipe of
Mucus lees that are
Replenishing the soon
Choked chambers of catarrh,

Not snore I heard, nor wheeze,
But something out of phase
With all of me: an owl
Out over Livingshayes.

In fact the birdcalls I
Can name are precious few.
Nightingales sang to me
Once, and I never knew.

Woodpigeon, meadowlark
With coo and trill augment
A gamut that remains
Indubitably scant.

And if, now I remember,
I lifted my head out of books

Enough to know one other
Call out of England: rooks . . .,

Is it not crows I mean
Or, what I am told is rare,
The death-conveying raven's
Croak through leaden air?

Bowels, adenoids,
Bald logic, brazen tongue . . .
Where is the other song the
Blackcap and wren have sung?

Cuckoo, plover, and owl:
A perilously confined
Aviary of sound for
One bedridden, or blind.

FARE THEE WELL

Bideford! Nothing will do
To make the place ring true
To its after-rain luminous presence
That day last summer, so
Precipitous, tempest-whipped
As that summer was to us two,
And as Bideford was also
That day we were there,

But embarkations: faces
Cheese-white in lamplight; lights
Dancing on blackness as
They rock away; oars are shipped,
'Ahoy!' and an answering growl,
And they climb aboard, and the wicker
Basket and bird-cage are
Hoist in; and the anchor is tripped.

Make what you will of the figure
Of outward, I cannot afford
To let you go, to unloose you
To that all-levelling
Hardship of ocean. See!
Some one has cast a hawser,
Some one has caught it. Wrapped
On a bollard, it checks, it is gripped.

Oh it is you I would check.
When it comes to the outward bound,
You are to be outstripped:
Farewell! I am far down the Sound,
Dwindled, my moorings slipped.
Somewhere by Barnstaple Bay
I have embraced you, I turn
Seaward. 'Farewell,' I say.

Because in the event
The hawser will not be bent
Nor gripped so handily, and
Goodbyes will be untoward
In some more sterilized place
Than Bideford, accept
This easy rehearsal: that when
The time comes, we be equipped.

GRACE IN THE FORE STREET
for Roy Gottfried

You saw the sunlight ripen upon the wall,
Inching daily as the year wore full.

Behind you as you worked at Shakespeare rose,
Slovenly shelved, the job-lot of my books

An image of my randomness. Across them
A bush in the yard on a fine cold morning throws

Calendared shadows wavering over Bishop
Wilson's Maxims, and Calvin excerpted in French:

One late lunge after piety; and one
Long ago at face-saving erudition.

Which motive, or what other one, procured
The Psalms of David in Arthur Golding's version

I wish I knew, and knew what price to put on
'The fear of the Lord is clean, and endureth for ever.'

I imagine you or another American friend
Explaining of me, when dead: 'Now in his day

As an Englishman . . .' But not my Englishness
Nor anything else about me ever ripened.

The English year revolves and brings to leaf
Great ancient oaks which then unleaf themselves;

In which there is no consolation nor,
The scale at best but saecular, grounds for hope.

A better hope let me from my unkempt
Bruised library bestow on you. It goes:

      'Who can understand his faults?
      Cleanse me from my secret faults . . .'

Unearned composures have been known to enter
A place of unfirm purpose and fleet shadows.

SOME FUTURE MOON
after Pasternak

Before me a far-off time arises
Far in the future. You,
Whoever you are, are mine;
This is to say I know you.

The sodium street-lights beam
On to a stonescape as
Remote from the Plymouth I know
As mine from Frobisher's.

You are a girl or a boy;
All the same, one of the few.
Whoever you are, you are mine;
This is to say I claim you.

This which I need to tell you
Quietly is none
Other than what the Tamar
Shines to the Eddystone.

Listen! For the lisp of
The waters at Admiral's Hard
Decayed in my day already
Now can scarcely be heard.

They neither shine nor sound
Unless in a little tune
I name both them and you
And set you under the moon.

Watch with me how the moon
Sinks on Mount Edgecumbe. Think
How many lovers' joys
With that moon rose, and sink.

And yet think also how,
Whatever your war-machines
And your machine-made songs,
These are unchanging scenes:

Because I say so, Mount
Edgecumbe's shelving ground
Crowds to the dropping down
Of warships outward bound;

Because I say so, you
Unknown sit with me here,
Your eyes a-shine because
I will it so, my dear.

You have this world no man
Nor man's machine can take
Away from you because
I made it for your sake.

OX-BOW

The time is at an end.
  The river swirled
Into an ox-bow bend, but now
  It shudders and re-unites:
  Adversary! Friend!

Adverse currents drove
  This pair apart.
A twin tormented throe embraced,
  Enisled between them, one
  Quadrant of earth, one grove.

Now for each other they yearn
  Across the eyot
That the peculiar flow of each
  Carved out, determined. Now,
  Now to each other they turn,

And it is past belief
  That once they forked;
Or that, upstream and bypassed, trees
  Mirrored in mid-reach still
  Break into annual leaf.

A LATE ANNIVERSARY

Constant the waterman
Skims the red water
Of sunset river,
Singing to Marian
The miller's daughter.

Wharf nor weir on this
Stretch of the river, it pours
Mournful and nebulous, Time's
Unseizable accomplice.

Sing to her, waterman.
Woo her unfaltering,
Constant as best you can,
Self-same by altering.

Your traffic is yourself:
The sidelong pour off a shelf
Or the popple about a stone.
It is what she would wish,
You have to think.

NO EPITAPH

No moss nor mottle stains
My parents' unmarked grave;
My word on them remains
Stouter than stone, you told me.

'Martyred to words', you have thought,
Should be your epitaph;
At other times you fought
My self-reproaches down.

Though bitterly once or twice
You have reproached me with how

Everything ended in words,
We both know better now:

You understand, I shall not
If I survive you care
To raise a headstone for
You I have carved on air.

PART TWO

UTTERINGS

(Bird)   To flex in the upper airs
To the unseen but known
Velocity of change
That both prevails and gives—
If anything that lives
That is able to know it, knows
Better to bend to the press
Of need, and so command it,
Him I envy, his
So much more strait duress.

(Salmon)   Pressures, pressures of water,
Of running water, because
As needs must downward driving,
Define imperatives.
If anything that lives
That is able to know it, knows
Better than I do the spine
Set taut against the grab
Of gravity, that thing knows
More happiness than mine.

(Man)   Making your own mistakes
And living the blame of them, making
The same ones time after time,
Which nobody forgives—
If anything that lives
That is able to know it, knows
A better happiness than
This—and he is Legion
That thinks he does—he is
Disranked from the branch of Man.

(Angel)   On us no pressures, none.
Adoration is

                    Not required, but what
                    Each one desirously gives.
                    If anything that lives
                    That is able to know it, knows
                    A better happiness, then
                    The frame of the world is askew;
                    I share the happiness
                    Of salmon, birds, and men.

(Sheepdog/   Knowing your own business,
Artist)   And such a delicate business;
                    Uttering it with the promptness
                    That such a knowledge gives—
                    If anything that lives
                    That is able to know it, knows
                    A better happiness
                    In his dog's life than this,
                    He is welcome to it; most,
                    I apprehend, know less.

SKELPICK

sub galea pastor iunctis pice cantat avenis,
proque lupo pavidae bella verentur oves

                         (*Ovid*, Tristia)

Below us all day, a mile away, in a flashing
Bend of the river a manikin is for manly
Sport not sustenance casting after and gaffing
The innocent salmon while over us all the clouds
Choir the incessant the variously lovely
Descants of shadows up and across the valley.

This is their glen, the Mackays of Strathnaver who
Were Hanoverian in the '45, who
Furnished the thin red line at Balaclava,
Whose sole exploit in earlier centuries was,
On a tribal foray against the Morays of Dornoch,
The spoliation of Scotland's prime cathedral.

Our childish companion, thinking excrement
Though it be of sheep is hilarious, is shouting
With laughter at me as I kick away sheep-shit
From the green knoll our rented cottage stands on,
Grease on the toe of my boot, me silently cursing
The mindless machines that they are, cropping and cropping.

Yet this is the one who, heaving himself from the small
Citroen he has required should stop, Good Shepherd
Labouring stiff-legged, cradles a possibly crippled
And certainly dam-spurned lamb, and then transports what
If it survives, survives only for slaughter
To a more sheltered dimple in the bracken.

One is not—I hope one is not—escaping the blood
Of the lamb, the excrement, the unsteady gait
After the dug that is always withdrawn, or the holy
Gaffed and gasping fish, the stinking fishwife
Raped beside the Dornoch Firth, by calling
For air, for air, for a distance, calling on

Tristia, the threads of a destiny woven
From a black fleece when a poet was born in Sulmona;
Tristia, the pipe pitch-bonded played
From under a war-bonnet over the shuddering flock;
Tristia, the beldam black Chaldeans'
Disastrous flocking torrent through the birch-trees.

STRATHNAVER

Dear language, English, whose
'Loyal' means the thing
A cairn by the road records
In clearwater green Strathnaver.

It honours the 83rd
Sutherland Highlanders, of
A Presbyterian clan,
Mustered in 1800.

Their sons and daughters were
Prised out to populate,
Far from the lonely shieling,
Canada and New Zealand.

And under Ben Loyal by
The ruined Clearances village
Of Scrabster Sutherland can
Heal me with space and silence.

A temporary remission,
Sour in any case. Hour
On hour of loyal service
Thus to be rewarded!

Spare from your frenzied mutters
Of 'Fool, fool, fool!' the men
Of the earliest 83rd,
Their cornfields gone to sheepwalks.

WINTER'S TALENTS
for Peter Scupham and Robert Wells

Nebulous, freezingly moist,
The need for a feelingful voice
Moves athwart and away
And upon us again, as we move
Northwest. The silvery stripes
Of mist come in and recede.
Past Hereford, each tree,
Grass-stalk and hedge stands dressed in
The need, a fur of rime.

Dee-side and Mersey-side
Lie up ahead, blocked off
In freezing fog. To them
The voice must speak. The rime
Dies off in the chemical reek.

Whose swag, whose chiselled cadence
Crusts, or whose coral, in
Garston, Halewood, Speke?
The voice, though, needs must speak.

Nor will it be content
With the abrupt sweet carol
Peeled against April brick,
The lyric; no, nor the dry
Incontestably true
Chirrup of pathos. New
Poets move across England.
Islanded, I salute them:
Elaborate talents of winter.

Marooned as I am in my own
Undoubtedly misread season
(Smoky noons I remember
In Liverpool), I salute the
Articulators of winter
Wonderlands. Delamere Forest's
Ramifications extort
Arpeggio and cadenza,
Too ornate for the *scouse*.

The need for a feelingful voice
Thwarts me, moves away,
Moves back. The bands of clear,
Then claustral weather gather
And then disperse. Rehearse,
Voices not mine, in England's
Interminable winter:
Sycamore, Tarporley, all
Intricate, cavernous splendour!

A LIVERPOOL EPISTLE

to J. A. Steers, Esq, author of
'The Coastline of England and Wales'

Alfred, this couple here—
My son, your daughter—are
Can we deny it? strangers
To both of us. Ageing, I
Find I take many a leaf
Out of the useful book
Of your behaviour. 'Prof.',
Your title for years, becomes
Me, or meets my need;
Mask for what heartaches, what
Uncertain, instantaneous
(Panicky sometimes)
Judgments how to behave in
This net we seem to have woven
Between us, or been caught in.

Under a rusty gown not
Actual but conjured
By our behaviour, what
In some diminished sense
Compromising situations we
Either escape, or handle! Still,
Today I was found at a loss,
Confronted with the local
University's stalwarts
Of a past age: Bernard Pares,
Oliver Elton, George
Sampson, Fitzmaurice-Kelly . . .
Not that they did not deserve
Attention, there in their daubed
Likenesses; but how?
What was required of 'the Prof.'?

In the event I managed
Well enough by my
Lenient expectations, but
I had such a sense of how

Tragical, one might say,
Our occupation is
Or may be. How
Beset it is, after all,
How very far from 'secluded',
This life of the scholar my son
And your daughter have followed us into!

It was explained to me,
For instance, there was one
Liverpool professor
Had had to be painted out
Of the group-portrait: Kuno
Meyer, Professor of German,
Whose notable devotion
To Ancient Irish took,
Come 1914, rather
A different colour. He
Declared himself for his Kaiser
Belligerently. And I
Must admit I am baffled:
Passion also has its
Claims upon us, surely;
Even the sort that is called,
Smirkingly, 'patriotic'.

Kenneth Allott, a poet
I think you will not have read,
Gave us ('I give you', he wrote)
'The riotous gulls and the men
Crumpled, hat-clutching, in the wind's
Rages, and the shifting river',
Giving us Liverpool. Here
Anyone must be prompted
To solemn reflections in
A wind that must seem like the wind
Of history, blowing the chemical
Reek out of Runcorn over
The eerily unfrequented,
Once so populous, Mersey.

Cold hearth of empire, whose
Rasping cinders bring
Our erudite concerns
Home to us, with such
Asperity! This is
Liverpool, one enormous
Image of dereliction
Where yet our children warm themselves
And so warm us. We too
Are netted into it—you
Known as the protector
Of England's coastline, and
I, supposedly
Custodian of that other
Line around England: verse.

This turns, of course. Yes, one
Verse-line turns into the next
As Rodney Street into a slum, or
Philologists into Prussians;
Turnings in time as your
Headlands and bays are turnings
In space. A bittersweet pleasure
At best one takes in these
Revolutions, reversals,
Verses, whereas
The veerings of a coastline
(Seen from a lowflying aircraft,
A coastal road or, best,
A coasting ship) must be
Experienced, I think, as
A solemn sweetness always.

As prose at its saddest is less
Sorrowful than verse is
Necessarily, so
Geography, I have long
Thought, must be a sweeter
Study than history; sweeter
Because less cordial, less

Of heartbreak in it. More
Human warmth, it follows,
Is possible or common
In Liverpool than in
Some spick-and-span, intact,
Still affluent city. So
The warmth of our children's household
For the time being persuades me.

WELL-FOUND POEM
'Of tried goodness, merit, or value—1887' (O.E.D.)

'We last of Yugo-Slav
Air Force. Please tell Alex.
we coming.' Signal received
21st April 1941 by
H.M.S. Chekla, towing,
somewhere south of Crete:
                                        'the
port quarter fairlead was
used, because *Desmoulea*
would be sheering
violently to starboard, and
if the fairlead should collapse, the
wire would bring up against
the portside of the steering-engine house
against which it was hoped
to hold it by a heavy
shackle (around the wire)
on a chain, with a tackle rove
to bowse it against the house.'

These are zones of language, zones
of the affecting universe
of Pepys's English prose and Dryden's verse.

The use of the slip-hook made it
impossible to

'freshen the nip'
of the towing wire
through the fairlead, but

so they managed that ship

        *

At Ostend's
evacuation, 'one
lady who threatened to go
into labour unless she sailed
in a destroyer.' This
'pleasure she was accorded but
without result.'
                By which
he means presumably
labour was not averted;
the lady was delivered
safely of a nine-
or eight-and-a-half pound fruit
of pleasure once accorded:
sturdy destroyer, male.

        *

'To re-establish tactics and
the skills of command . . .'

precision-guided missiles
favour it; so far from
'push-button warfare', the problem
is, with them,
no longer to
'hit early and keep on hitting'
but knowing what it is
you hit, and what happens to it;

as for instance Mr
Wilson, Commissioned Gunner,

'had his face blown away';
'unable to move him', nor
'had I the time',
'left him covered with a blanket.'

*

We last of Yugo-Slav
Air Force. Please tell
Alexandria,
Athens, Rome
in a violet light

we coming. Oberleutnant
Prell is coming, and
Commissioned Gunner Wilson
is coming, and

tactics and the skills
of command are coming and

these are zones of language and

we would not have it otherwise. The cities
form and re-form in the violet light, and

his face had been blown away and
we would not have it otherwise, destroyers

male, and tell Alex. We
coming, we always coming:

'. . . these brave men . . .'

ARTIFEX IN EXTREMIS

In memoriam Howard Warshaw

Let him rehearse the gifts reserved for age
   Much as the poet Eliot did, but more
   Than thirty-five years after : . . . Rending rage
Discountenanced by his Church, the rent and sore
   Patient nods under gin or seconal
   Or his small fame, such drugs. His visitor,
The one and only in this hospital,
   Is nurse and woman. Time and time again
   She brings her numbing serum, whom to call
A button's by his bed. He calls her when,
   Ashamed, he feels his practised self-control
   Slipping a notch. Hotly he asks her then:
'Is there no choice? Am I to sell my soul
   Short, or fake it, for my nearest kin
   Forever, till I die?' Prompt on the whole
She brings her priceless needleful of guilt,
   Oblivion, and equality; his rôle
   Is possum, playing possum to the hilt.

The hilt, though, is a long way down and in;
   The whole blade is before it, going deep
   Bleeding and shearing. Though the mottled skin
Knits up and shines, the legless cries in his sleep
   For pain in the limb aborted. There was once,
   Torturing to remember, in that steep
Slope off to nowhere, stamping-ground and stance,
   Foothold, some hard earth under. He discerns
   Still many a cherished, hard-earned eminence
Loom from his past, on all of which by turns
   He took his stand. No need to specify.
   There is not one of them that now he spurns;
On all that ring of hills his drowsing eye
   Sees his young self still model rectitude
   Erect and certain. Clear against the sky
Above his drug-dimmed but still savage mood,
   Seen but by him, the things that he has held by
   Unchangeably enforce his solitude.

His arrogance is terrible to no one
   More than to him. It is incurable.
   The enormity of it ramrods bone on bone
When he stands up for anything at all,
   Rending both it and him. No palliation
   In trusting to posterity, at call
No longer for belated vindication;
   The future, if it comes (as he is not
   Sure that it will), will in his estimation
Be more obtuse, not less. His work is what
   Stands, but as if on Easter Island, rude
   And enigmatic effigies, a lot
Unsold at history's auction. When of crude
   Unlettered clergy Thomas Cranmer's prose
   Demands too much, what but desuetude
Attends one's best? This being what he knows,
   His own sick say-so and presumption can
   Alone sustain the artificer in the man.

Then why, he asks himself (his self-contempt
   Half self-pity), of late these reams on reams
   Addressed to a young kinsman? To attempt,
Having no heirs, to write one's will—it seems
   The enforced sell-out: exegetes pre-empt
   Prophecies, polemics serve for dreams,
And pedagogue supplants protagonist,
   As rhetoric, action. Always in the event
   One must, despite the lacerating twist
Of disbelief, limp to a testament
   Too shrill for dignity. Of late he's missed
   That most—the dignity. A low sun lent
Once or twice, his monumental forms
   Upon the hill-tops just the effect he meant:
   Scrutable, yet unfathomable. Norms
Of expectation (anxious, confident,
   His kinsman's face . . .) obscure them; one performs
   Simply such things, intent, without intent.

For the most part now he drifts, his conduct as
   Considerate as has come to be expected,

Querulous seldom. His *superbia* has
Been at such pains to ravage undetected
   (And swelled the more) that now he practises
   Unthinkingly the long ago perfected
Deceit of warming to the common touch,
   Much-loved, attentive. That too he has made
   A point of, staunchly—not to ask, for such
As he is, special licences. Betrayed
   By that pretence of unpretension, much
   As now he may regret the terms of trade
He fixed himself, he has to acquiesce
   When he perceives his own dear things are weighed
   And shelved at market-prices. To confess
The work that would, he thought, speak for itself
   Has not, comes hard. Benumbed, he stands himself,
   With all his other pieces, on the shelf.

'A good life,' he will tell me, 'though I wish . . .'
   And so on—much what anyone might say.
   Blind to his own case? Or this queerer fish
That terrifies me, reading him today
   Into myself tomorrow—which one thumbs
   The bedside button, and no woman comes?

THE BENT

Thinking how it is
   too late to undertake
      one more dutiful office
against my bent ('the grain',
   I called it once), too late
      to make as much as can
be made of Paul Celan or
   Zukofsky's 'A', and
      recalling how I met
the latter, reluctantly though
   rewardingly in the event,
      and how he is dead, I am left

with the conjecture poets
    have treated me with as much
        compassionate gentleness as
we might ascribe to centaurs
    finding within their troop
        either a man or a horse.

When I consider these
    whose operations are
        not beyond me but
as it were beside me
    in an alternative cosmos
        I do not envy them.

CATULLUS ON FRIENDSHIP

*'Cancel, Catullus, the expectancies of friendship
Cancel the kindnesses deemed to accrue there . . .'*
                       (tr. Peter Whigham)

It must make a great difference, having friends.
    Yeats had Pound and Pound had Yeats, and Frost
Had, briefly, Edward Thomas. It must make
    A world of difference, having trusted friends
And trustworthy—eh, my Lampadius?

It must make all the difference, having friends
    To be dealt with cleanly, honestly—must it not,
Busy Lampadius? Friends who are not too busy
    To recognize the claims one has on them,
The vise one has them in—that too of course.

A world, a world of difference, my
    Never quite trusted and yet far too trusted
Friend, Lampadius . . . One must rub along.
    Just so, just so; the debts of friendship must,
Given the state of the market, be adjusted.

Lampadius, you're a poet; a busy one,
    And not half bad. Whichever god you sing

Or speak to, it's a lonely business; if
   To no god but a friend, it's lonelier;
But loneliest when there's no one there but 'readers'.

What puzzles or intrigues me, then, is how
   Your busy-ness refuels. In our youth
Mere self-advancement is a sufficient target:
   The sort of fame that's 'being talked about'.
What kept you going when you'd tired of that?

A secret, and you'll keep it. I don't know
   Whether or not to envy you the possession
Of such pure fuel as it seems I never
   Had, or have lost. My name for it was 'friendship';
Which can't be right, I think when I think of you.

'Kindred souls'—a prettily old-fashioned
   Extravagant name for what we had and have,
A competition between siblings. Such
   Olympian squabbles as that phrase clears up,
Which exercised the ancestors so direly!

Cleared up, acknowledged, cleared away . . . And yet
   The gods help friendship, since the life-force holds
No stake in it. Lampadius, what I
   Mean to say is I can't sing or speak
When friends and kindred can be sold downriver.

TWO FROM IRELAND

(1) 1969, Ireland of the Bombers

Blackbird of Derrycairn,
Sing no more for me.
Wet fields of Dromahair
No more I'll see

Nor, Manorhamilton,
Break through a hazelwood

In tufted Leitrim ever.
That's gone for good.

Dublin, young manhood's ground,
Never more I'll roam;
Stiffly I call my strayed
Affections home.

Blackbird of Derrycairn,
Irish song, farewell.
Bombed innocents could not
Sing half so well.

Green Leinster, do not weep
For me, since we must part;
Dry eyes I pledge to thee,
And empty heart.

(2) 1977, Near Mullingar
for Augustine Martin

'Green Leinster, never weep
   For me, since we must part.
Dry eyes I pledge to thee,
   And empty heart.'

Travelling by train
   —For I am a travelling man—
Across fields that I laid
   Under this private ban,

I thought: a travelling man
   Will come and go, here now
And gone tomorrow, and
   He cannot keep a vow.

Forsworn, coming to Sligo
   To mend my battered past,
I thought: It must be true;
   The solder cannot last.

But, dear friends, I could weep.
    Is it the bombs have made
Old lesions knit, old chills
    Warm, and old ghosts be laid?

Atrociously, such changes!
    The winning gentleness
Gentler still, and even
    The poets not so reckless.

Twenty-five years at least
    Higher up the slope
That England plunges down:
    That much grounds for hope.

Easy pronouncements from
    The stranger, as he leaves!
The truth is, he was home
    —Or so he half-believes.

PENELOPE

    And so, the retraction.
Time for it: after much
Effusion, undertow.

    And all right, so;
The year wears, and the worn
Capacities, coarsening,

    Honour the thing
Beyond them, the transaction
Clinched lately, clinched no more.

    Charity for
A while; then, grace withdrawn;
The flow, and then the ebb.

What wove the web
Now frays it, with as much
Devotion in each breath.

Long-absent Death
Veers in the offing; nears
And goes off, to-and-fro.

And all right, so;
This being out of touch
Alone tests constancy.

It is to be
A prey to hopes and fears;
Fears mostly, as is right.

In landfall light
The faithless absentee,
Death, assays our loves.

Though nothing removes
The weight of it, when the year's
Circuit spells: 'dry',

Not asking why
But blessing it, is to see
At last impunity.

PART THREE

DEVIL ON ICE

Called out on Christmas Eve for a working-party,
Barging and cursing, carting the wardroom's gin
To save us all from sin and shame, through snow,
The night unclear, the temperature sub-zero,
                Oh I was a bombardier
                For any one's Angry Brigade
That Christmas more than thirty years ago!

Later, among us bawling beasts was born
The holy babe, and lordling Lucifer
With him alas, that blessed morn. And so
Easy it was, I recognize and know
                Myself the mutineer
                Whose own stale bawdry helped
Salute the happy morn, those years ago.

Red Army Faction could have had me then;
Not an intrepid operative, but glib,
A character-assassin primed to go,
Ripe for the irreplaceable though low
                Office of pamphleteer.
                Father of lies, I knew
My plausible sire, those Christmases ago.

For years now I have been amenable,
Equable, a friend of law and order,
Devil on ice. Comes Christmas Eve . . . and lo!
A babe we laud in baby-talk. His foe
                And ours, not quite his peer
                But his antagonist,
Hisses and walks on ice, as long ago.

ADVENT

Some I perceive, content
And stable in themselves
And in their place, on whom
One that I know casts doubt;
Knowing himself of those
No sooner settled in
Than itching to get out.

I hear and partly know
Of others, fearless and
Flinging out, whom one
I know tries to despise;
Knowing himself of those
No sooner loosed than they
Weeping sue for the leash.

Some I see live snug,
Embosomed. One I know
Maunders, is mutinous,
Is never loved enough;
Being of those who are
No sooner safely lodged
They chafe at cherishing.

Some I know who seem
Always in keeping, whom
One I know better blusters
He will not emulate;
Being of those who keep
At Advent, Whitsuntide,
And Harvest Home in Lent.

Some who are his kin
Have strewn the expectant floor
With rushes, long before
The striding shadow grows
And grows above them; he,
The deeper the hush settles,
Bustles about more business.

The eclipse draws near as he
Scuttles from patch to shrinking
Patch of the wintry light,
Chattering, gnashing, not
Oh not to be forced to his knees
By One who, turned to, brings
All quietness and ease.

Self-contradictions, I
Have heard, do not bewilder
That providential care.
Switch and reverse as he
Will, this one I know,
One whose need meets his
Prevents him everywhere.

HAVING NO EAR

Having no ear, I hear
And do not hear the piano-tuner ping,
Ping, ping one string beneath me here, where I
Ping-ping one string of Caroline English to
Tell if Edward Taylor tells
The truth, or no.

Dear God, such gratitude
As I owe thee for giving, in default
Of a true ear or of true holiness,
This trained and special gift of knowing when
Religious poets speak themselves to God,
And when, to men.

The preternatural! I know it when
This perfect stranger—angel-artisan—
Knows how to edge our English Upright through
Approximations back to rectitude,
Wooing it back through quarter-tone
On quarter-tone, to true.

Mystical? I abjure the word, for if
Such faculty is known and recognized
As may tell sharp from flat, and both from true,
And I lack that capacity, why should I
Think Paradise by other light than day
Sparkled in Taylor's eye?

SILOAM

for Clyde Binfield
'By cool Siloam's shady rill' (Heber)

Arkansaw's westernmost county
Is dry; we nip back over
The out-of-town stateline for
Liquor in Oklahoma.

In the next one, 'wet', a drive-in
Announces 'Kinky Ladies';
A shack says 'Modern Massage',
Not open yet for trading.

A titter: 'This is what
Free Churchmen mean by a *felt*
Religion? We are, are we not,
At the heart of the Bible Belt?

We are. This is Siloam
Springs. Once off the highway,
We walk in the 1930s,
Provincial yesterday:

The two or three blocks we walk
Of dark-brick downtown, sparsely
Frequented, could be almost
How I remember Barnsley,

Except for this river, whatever
River it is, scarved round

The whole small so-called 'city',
Flowing without a sound.

Green, deep-bushed green, the waters
And weir under the hill;
A little park by cool
Siloam's shady rill

Recalls in bronze the appalling
Highest the waters rose
Once, and the devastation—
By God's will, we suppose.

Imagine a deacon of
Drowned bottomlands, his brows
Sternly, despairingly knitted,
In the next county's whorehouse

Drowning himself! This country
Was lately and not completely
Humanized; here the dooms
Come suddenly and stately.

It is thus I perceive this lady,
Hatted and gloved, advancing,
Two grandchildren in tow,
Her eyes on us bright and dancing.

And this is on the bridge
Under the hanging wood,
Feeling precarious over
Siloam's fateful flood.

A CHRISTIAN HERO
(J. H. Lefroy. Canada, 1843-44)

'Not the action of rowing:
Intentness, intelligent will
In the crewmen of the canoes,
Facing the way they go in . . .'

Who is this candid traveller, whose
Aquiline Christian mind pursues
First, at *Portage deux Rivières*,
Distinctions sensuous yet severe?
Who was it first, between
Saskatchewan and Churchill
Rivers, where bare hills occur,
Asked himself what it could mean
For rock, mere unclothed rock, to stir
Such happiness? What questioner
Knew his idlest questions thus
The most momentous, least of use?

Whose the observances
The observations? Whose
Victorian rectitude
(He kept his sabbaths clear)
As soon would reason why about
The burden of a freighted mood
As what threw compass-readings out
Nearing the North? Who hunted down
Painfully the Magnetic Pole
Clocked through the months? The calendars
Of Keble's and of Humboldt's years,
Church's and Science's, confined
Doubly this least constricted mind.

Whose this enfranchised soul?
A much committed man's,
And straitly laced;
Would save the Cree for Christ.

AN ANGLICAN LADY
in memoriam Margaret Hine

Flattered at having no
less an authority than
Richard Hooker named
for my correction, I

had drawn, before I knew it, the
notepaper towards me for
the reference (Book Five:
sixty, three) when, live,
you sprang before me, Margaret.

                              I had chanced,
brought perhaps by sortilege or some
diviner leading, on
a sheet of your, the secretary's
notepaper. Oh my
poor Margaret, after how many
years, and since Hooker how
many centuries, does this
sad clod encounter, not in books but in
East Anglian blowing mornings, his
and Hooker's and your own, your decorous, God!

MANDELSTAM'S HOPE FOR THE BEST

(1) The Case Against
'man must be the hardest thing on earth'

Stout and well-knit in fact,
But avian was the impression;
Skimming compacted bird-brain.
Everyone's ikon, martyred;
In life, not altogether
Lifelike, unless as a bird.

A bird that lives on bees!
No more classical emblem,
Gentile or Jew, will the age
That martyred him permit us
Than his own chirr of bees from
Stringent and high Taigetos;

Honeybees dried and strung,
Hard pellets, into a necklace

Of Russian words that he twines
And twines before us while
The deep blue Ovidian twilight
Purples internal exile.

Hard! As nails? No, harder;
Mailed with an unaltering
Assurance of redemption,
The Cross his *passe-partout*
To broad Parnassian fields
Under enamelled blue.

(2) Son of Isaac

Ram caught in Stalin's thicket!
Rigged trials, typhus . . . Yahweh
Was Georgian, the 'I AM'
Expert in quickset mazes.

Though it is hard to say,
A Mandelstam's
Assurance of redemption
Huddles distress away.

The one-sided trade of man
With God has more of drama
Than his Parnassian
Enamel could gloss over.

His cupola, his cradle,
His ring (oh it is ringing
Home so bronze and true!)
All this settles nothing.

Much though it stirs us, still it
Forecloses on our hope
Too brutally. A harder
Trade earns wider scope

Than his so beautiful ring
Of memory, love and culture.
Wrestling with the angel
Pries the cupola open.

Jacob, the haunted child
Of him this surrogate
Saved by dying for,
Will not be reconciled.

(3) Hope Not Abandoned

Hope so abstracted as
towards no temporal end
but 'a mode of address to facts,
to the world and to its persons',
however it be attested
by every grace of behaviour
sought for and found in language,
had better agree to be called
a living contradiction.

To avoid abuse of terms,
let poets say they are hopeless,
and this at whatever cost
in the self-approved dissenter's
brilliance of negation.
Better thus than to fox
ourselves by appropriating
a cardinal term to actions
by which, ourselves, we are baffled.

The alternative to the degrading
gibberish of the Gross
National Product is
known to, and hated by,
those who most gibber. It
is not the historical Church
but whatever asserts our ends

are, and therefore our hopes,
metaphysical, like our terrors.

(4) Sonnet

As massive and dispensable as sculpture
Bees, dancing, point and utter their location.
Cotillions interspinning; monumental
Gossamer build-up of gnats' spiring wings
Punctuates space, commands it, by the river
Ephemerally, some evening. So a fly
Moves on the arm of Rodin's thinker with
No less weight than his effigy moves on earth.

Carve in that stone, Acmeist! Parian marble
You like to think so cold is all a-zing
With momentary fevers, and the scarp
Of language you would quarry, poet, whirls
Indeterminately shapely in
Helix on nebulous helix, not to be netted.

(5) Of his Armenia
'Ararat has drunk the air' (Mandelstam)

Self-aggrandizing to say, and yet it is true:
When I went there in 1942,
Though I had read few of the books, and no one knew
All of the facts, the torn-apart suffering hung,
Suffusion or deposit of the years,
Glittering like mica or like tears
Around the Arctic toe-hold where we clung,
North of Murmansk, on to his mother-bear Russia.

Nothing was less like miasma. Mountainy air
It was, though there were no mountains. There was one
Mountain in our sense of it, hanging there,
Not to be dealt with by guides or expert advice,
No holiday chalets upon it nor excavators'

Trolley-lines disused among flowers at Delphi,
But there at our backs: a mountain that cast no shadow
Indeed, but excess of light—the Arctic ice.

Such he one time imagined, a serener
Than earth-bound mountain spilling the ice-flow Grace,
As pure and polar as music of Palestrina
He said, and pointed—where I cannot follow
Not now nor then, having too poor an ear.
Ox-like obtuse (though there are Armenian churches
Ox-like, he says), what can I do with a clue
Harder to grasp than what it sets out to construe:

The Eucharist? I had no way to know
The far other end of his lands, nor how he had
For those without an ear, without a head
For freezing heights, climbed an accessible mountain
As full of Grace, vineyarded, colour of ochre:
Ararat, earthenware mountain. It would be long
Before I could learn from him and in part for myself
The God-given mercy and warmth of terra-cotta.

THREE BEYOND

In memoriam Michael Ayrton, Claude Simpson, William Partridge

Judgment occurs, but is not
For the judged of much importance.
Who cares for the rank in which he
Utters his adorations?

Thinking of the blessèd
Company of the saints and
The army of martyrs, I find that
One friend of three absolves me.

Two artists and one scholar
I think of; and it is one

Of the artists, the less acknowledged,
Who comes through, solacing most.

One has to understand that
Over there, over the last
Hurdle, the race is over;
No one there is competing.

One has to understand that
The ranks, the armies-are
Indeed there ranged in order,
But an order all will acknowledge.

Heavenly smiles from the two that,
Prayed to, gave limited comfort;
Delighted I should have reached to
Him of the highest standing.

A GARLAND FOR RONSARD

(1)

Green eyes from under cornsheaf curls
    Dart out at him, belated
Masks of alarming Orpheus, gaping
    And uncoordinated.

In dreams, in dreams . . . It is not true
    They haunt the familiar Loir,
Capering their black classics of
    Provence and Navarre.

Why then should laurels above the acclaimed
    Brow and the haggard face
Attest a restive Athenian, half
    In love with incult Thrace?

(2)
Dieu les tient agitez . . .

These—of whom only four or five are known
To have existed, mostly Greek—aspire
Not to the style of poet, but the stele
Erected in some secret glade nearby
Ancestral acres. Into these the god's
Sizzling probe pricks insecurity
At every turn. The common talk esteems them—
Not without some complacency—'unsound',
Countryside crazies. It is thought they've much
Traffic with fairies, nymphs; with any not
Quite human *leman*, leaping the vales, woods, mountains.

(3)
Antres, et vous fontaines . . .

Caverns, and you fountains
That off the beetling mountains
Slide to this humbler place
    With stealing pace;

You also, forests; waves
whose gipsying current laves
These fields; woods, banks that bend
    Each side, attend:

When Heaven and my hour
Shall rule I be no more,
Reft from my happy stay
    In common day,

I make it your affair
No journeyman shall square
Marble to make ornate
    My entombed state.

Let my remains be hid
Under no marble lid,
But rather let the screen
    Be evergreen.

And earth-engendered from
Me may ivy come,
In which I may be wound
    Round and around.

The braided vine embellish
My sepulchre, and flourish
To cast on every side
    A speckled shade.

To that place shall repair
On my name-day each year

The droves of cattle and
    The drovers' band;

When, having made their fit
Oblation as is meet,
These words to the isle i' the river
    Shall they deliver:

'How widely are you known,
Who serve as tomb for one
Of whom the universe
    Intones the verse!

Whom Rancour, what is more,
In life consumed not, nor
Reduced to supplicate
    For grants the great;

Who'd not re-introduce
The aphrodisiac use
Of drams, nor yet have part
    In mages' art;

But rather to our own
Plains made the Sisters known,
Bending the grass to their
    Songs in the air.

For on his strings he knew
To winnow out such true
Accordance as adorns
    Us, and our lawns.

May the sweet manna rain
For ever on this terrain
That is his tomb, which let
    The May dews wet.

Grass crowns, and waters ring,
The site; the grasses spring

Green, and the fluctuant wave
    Brims round his grave.

To him we, mindful how
Glory redounds, will bow
As if to Pan each year
    Our foreheads here.'

Thus shall the rustic troop
Declare, while many a cup
Shall pour its votive flood,
    Milk and lamb's blood,

On me, who shall by then
Be gone to that domain
Where the blest spirits roam
    And make their home.

Not hailstorms nor the snow
Upon those quarters blow,
Nor ever thunder dare
    Break on them there;

But an immortal green
Adorns the constant scene,
And constant through all time
    Spring's at the prime.

Every solicitude
Kings care for, these elude:
They raze no world, the faster
    The world to master;

But live as brothers do,
And though they are dead pursue
The self-same trades they plied
    Before they died.

There I shall hear his lyre,
Alcaeus's, strung to ire;

And Sappho's chords, that fall
    Sweetest of all.

How much must those who long
Attend the diffusive song
Rejoice to be of those
    Who hear echoes

That the incumbent rocks
Rock back at, while what blocks
Old Tantalus fails for once
    His pain to advance!

Lyre! Sweet lyre! What more
Can heal our heartaches or
So far on us impose
    We hear repose?

   (4)
End to Torment

At Ste Madeleine de Croixval,
housebound with gout, four sonnets;
October—
        'dusty air . . .
September's yellow gold that mingled fair
With green and rose tint on each maple bough
Sulks into deeper browns'.
              He died in that
same year at the other priory, St Cosme.

Hélène, Cassandre, Yseult
Is-hilda, Undine, 'O
swallow, my sister'—look
out for whom you
fatuously endow, though
posterity fail not desert perhaps.

Frenetic and protean
(One noted: double chin!)

'perched like a bird at dusk',
huge eyes, thin shoulders; or
the strapping one perched, shoes off
at the foot of his bunk. They are
no good, you know, these girls.

What did he write?
'Myrrh and olibanum',
gum-resin from incisions
in South Arabia: *dendron*,
cecily, chervil—and
AMOR, the palindrome ROMA.
Backward or forward it read
the same: she-wolf.

'There is a mellow twilight 'neath the trees
Soft and hallowed as is a thought of thee . . .'
'Whisper in the murmurous twilight where
I met thee mid the roses of the past
Where you gave your first kiss in the last . . .'
And which of them all did he, oh well,
'love'?
            The Lady Loba.

   (5)

Living without Marie
Makes him, since he has tried,
Know what it is to live
Without the one illusion
That he has lived inside.

France, Orphic Greece Renewed,
Himself the Orpheus—all
Farrago, all mistaken.
Yes, but to be by her
He staked it on, forsaken . . .

Of course not celibate
For all his tonsure. Still

Rossignols' orisons
Could hardly compensate
For never having sons.

Though how much that amounts to
How could he calculate?
One has not, or one has,
Sons; and no one can
Know both alternatives.

Forget the brigade of his fellows
And the adoring pupils.
What he lacks in the end
Is not the bedmate even,
But the sulky spitfire friend.

(6)

Génèvres hérissez, et vous, houx espineux . . .

Bush-bristling juniper and you the thorn-
Enjoying holly, one the desert's guest
And one the thicket's; ivy-cover drawn
Across waste caves; sand-spiring spouts and freshets;
    Pigeons that sip at them; you mourning doves
In your unending widowhood; nightingales
Who day-long night-long in appealing jargon
Rehearse the unvaried versicles of your loves;

    And you with the red throat, non-indigenous swallow—
If you should see *la Cara* in this Spring
Abroad for flowers, parting the young grasses,
    Tell her from me I hope for nothing now
From her, no favours. Cut the suffering:
As well be dead as carry on like this.

'PASTOR ERRANTE'

for Robert Pinsky

'And you, Enscaldunac?' (Mary Austin, The Flock)

When you were explaining America, Robert, you did not
    —Why should you?—explain
To your small daughter there had been a time when the *pastor*,
    Meaning the shepherd in
Many tongues though not as it happens in Basque,
    Roamed the Sierra Nevada.

It would, you must see, have made a difference: not
    To have those alarmingly non-
Communicating Swedes or German-speaking
    Bohemians on
The Willa Cather prairies for your girl
    To grow wide-eyed at;

But instead in Inyo County Mary Austin's
    Long-gone shepherds who might
As well have been Hebrew or Greek or Sicilian as
    What they were largely—Basques,
Speaking their own impenetrable language
    And yet familiar.

What we seem to be speaking of, if you agree with me, is
    A sort of utterance
Made from out of earshot, the wonderful surely
    Lexicons of gesture
Though of implements also—Californian shepherds
    Even had crooks!

Is it only to us, and not to our children, that
    A shepherd's crook, which I
Doubt I have ever seen, is more comforting than
    That appalling threshing-machine
You imagined in which, like Berryman waving, your hobo
    Pitched head-first?

Imagine an America that was what
    At one time I infer

It might have been: the West not lost, a true
  Pastoral, sheep-bells ringing.
Would it have made a difference? Would it not, and
  Why do you think so?

I do not expect an answer. The lord Hermes,
  Tutelary deity
Of shepherds, no doubt patronizes also
  Hermetic poetry, ours:
Wherein we ask unanswerable questions
  To what man's profit?

Errant through why not America? although Asia
  Is what Leopardi
Too plangently imagined, that much nearer
  The god's faint trace. And

        'Moon',
    He starts out, bald as that, '*what are you doing*
    There in the sky? Unspeaking moon,
    What are you about? You come
    Up in the evening, and you go
    Looking at deserts; then you stop, stand still.
    What is this all about? Are you
    Pleased to be pacing these eternal alleys?
    Don't you get bored? Or is it
    Still to your liking, looking down on these
    Glens of ours? Ah well, your life is
    Much like a shepherd's. Up he gets before
    Dawn, and moves out
    His sheep to pasture, sees to
    Folds, to water, fodder; then,
    Tired out, snores through the evening:
    Hopes for no more, ever. Tell
    Me, you moon: what is it worth to
    The shepherd, this life of his,
    And what to you, your life? Tell me
    The ends they move to: his brief, vagrant life
    And yours, unending.'

One perceives the question
    Looks for a no more
Reassuring answer than the worst we might
    Frame to alarm
Our daughters with, or else ourselves reflecting
    About our daughters. Where
Does it come in then, the incongruous sweetness?
    From oaten reed and
Lyrical tortoise-shell? I wouldn't knock it,
    I tell myself
And tell you, Robert: Sicily, ancient Hebron,
    We cull their honeycombs.
Why should we not? And he goes on:

                                          'An old

White and unable man,
Half-dressed at best, and shoeless,
A heavy bundle toted on his shoulders,
By mountains, valleys and sharp boulders
In wind, in storm, and when it
Heats up and afterwards freezes,
Keeps going, keeps, keeps going
Through streaming and through standing
Waters he falls, he gets up, bit by bit
Quickens his going, he quickens it, torn and
Bloody; and at last he reaches
To where the road and where so much
Overstraining stretched him to: to the
Hair-raising gulch where he,
Oblivious, pitches in. Immaculate moon,
Immaculate, virginal, such
The life of the dying, the mortal, the set to deadward.'

    Now why should we,
I ask you, derive any measure of consolation
    From such a cry, or from
The way of life that past all responsible doubt it
    Faithfully utters? I
Cannot explain why a pastoral life that I could not
    Pursue should

Figure for me as, however uncouth, still
    Human and proper, as
(To take a plain instance) the life of a rabble-rousing
    Activist, though
He too has his classical prototype, the *rhetor*,
    Emphatically is not.

> *'A man is born to*
> *Painstaking, and his very*
> *Birth is in hazard to death.*
> *Trouble and worry are*
> *The first things probe him. In his very*
> *Setting out Mother and Father*
> *Take on to console him*
> *For having been born. And then*
> *As he starts to grow up, the one*
> *Takes over from the other*
> *In heartening him, to come to*
> *Terms with his human status.*
> *This is the best that parents*
> *Can do for their children. But why*
> *If that is the case donate them*
> *To daylight in the first place? Why*
> *Hold up at all in a life that*
> *Crowds to such consolation?*
> *If life is all misadventure,*
> *Why does it keep going*
> *Inside us? Untouchable moon,*
> *This is the life of mortals, but*
> *Mortal is what you are not;*
> *And what I say perhaps*
> *Very little concerns you.*
>   *To you, you solitary, you*
> *Moon, eternal vagrant*
> *Brooding upon yourself, perhaps this*
> *Life on earth comes clear, and this*
> *Undergoing of ours, this breathing out*
> *Of sighs, all this*
> *That is, and happens; also what*
> *Happens in this*

Dying, this ultimate
Changing of colour in the way we look,
This perishing off
The earth, this coming clean of
All settled habits and good neighbourhood.'

Skip a bit then, and:

'So it is that I
Cogitate, both on the grand
Immeasurable heavenly mansions and
On the uncountable kin. And then,
After so long on the stretch,
Coping with so many
Each and every first celestial motion
And each terrestrial, every one of them turning,
Turning only to return to
Where they started from, it is then I
Can find no use nor fruit of it. To you,
Undying bride, no doubt it is
Comprehensible. But this I
Both recognize and feel:
From the eternal turnings
Around, and my own unstable
Being, whatever may come of
Good or satisfying is
For some one else. For me, my life is evil.'

What sort of a frigid monster would one have to
    Be, to derive consolation
From such a confession? How to deflect, by any
    Muster of formulaic
Muting properties, crook and staff, the brute
    Drive, and the justified pain?

What should we be, will we be, have we been doing, persuading
    Our daughters they would be safe with
For instance a hulking great villain once, flagging us down,
    Sheepskin over his shoulder in
Arcady if you believe it, in rain, and not without menace
    Cadging a smoke?

The justified pain, the justified brute . . . So
    Telling our daughters
Of pastoral idylls, what we might mean is this:
    There are some failures in
Life, and I mean in a life-long effort, one would not
    Soon confess to, Robert; and
Knowledge, foreknowledge of them (they are not the
                            shepherd's
    Ineluctable hardships, though
One found no way to elude them)—such foreknowledge
    Is, you would surely agree,
What none of us has the heart or the gall to transmit to
    Our gullible daughters. Isn't
That the best reason for rubbing their dear snub-noses
    Into a shepherd's mishaps?

SUMMER LIGHTNING

for Seamus Heaney, in imitation of Ronsard

> *'L'argument du Comicque est de toutes saisons.'*

Heaney, one can get word-perfect at
Any profession. Law needs working at
But can be mastered; practice of Physic makes
Practitioners perfect; grind is what it takes
To come by effective public speaking or
Become a consummate philosopher;
Even the best computer-wallahs know it's
Close study counts. It's not like that with poets . . .
   Perfect is what the Art has up to now
Not been, and won't be, here; God won't allow
That much credit to Humanity.
Unfinished as we know ourselves to be,
Earthy by definition, could we reach,
Ever, to perfect energy of speech?
   The gift of poetry is like the fire
Seen of a summer's night: flames that transpire
Like a foreboding over a river, over
A field, or again there, flickering, hover

To silhouette some plume on a far coppice
Become a sacred grove. This randomness
Makes people jumpy; seeing the weird flame,
Souls for a moment batter against their frame.
And in the end it gutters down, all this
Dumb foundry-blast of clarification is
Suddenly dull, and then it dies away.
Because it's not predictable day by day
But jumps from place to place, never at rest,
No country gets this migrant on request
Or is bequeathed her. Some emergent state
Is (so one hopes) her current favourite.
    And so no Hebrew, Greek nor Roman hand
Can handle all of poetry on demand.
Germany she has visited, she advances
Her claim to England's coasts, to Scotland's, France's,
Vaulting over, wheeling, taking great
Pleasure in picking some unlooked-for state
And some unlikely person. The bright flare
Illuminates some province here or there,
Then just as soon evaporates in air.
The Muse, in short, is international;
She is put up by, she puts up with, all;
Peculiar to no property, no one breed.
But whom she picks on, him she clips indeed.
    Take me now, Heaney—and let this suffice:
If I have made it, it was at a price
Such as I'm not sure others would have paid.
What I know is this art of mine has flayed
Me, and still does. I'm skinned! So, after one
Death let me have another one, to stun
Into insensibility. I've had much
Fun in this life; and yet the undulant touch
Of the Parnassian flood, Permessus, meant
I would be, as I have been, somnolent,
Unhandy, useless; worse, I must admit
I cannot give it up, I'm slave to it.
    I am opinionated and embittered,
Inconsiderate, gruff, low-spirited,
Pleased and displeased at once, huffy and raw;

And yet I fear God, fear the Crown, the Law,
Am spry enough by nature, cordial,
Content to have vexed nobody at all.
So there you have me, Heaney . . . I suppose
All of our lot have vices much like those.
     Now if Calliope, to make up for this,
Had made me better than the best there is,
Star pupil in her class, star of the show,
Then all these feelings that I undergo
I could put up with. But it isn't so;
Since I'm at best a halfway poet here,
I'd rather like some less godlike career.
     Two sorts of business flourish on that hill
Of the nine Lóvelies. One's compatible
With those who like to say that they 'compose',
Who tot up and keep tallies, who dispose
These many verse-lines here; beneath them, those.
(Tell off fourteen, and bless me, you've a sonnet,
Its subject: Time, a poet's reflections on it.)
By 'versifiers' (which these are) is meant
That verse on verse is all that they invent,
All cold too, ice-cold. Brought to bed, these brought
Out some small slice of life—which they abort!
Such verse does best as drapery for a pound
Of sugar or rice, ground ginger, screwed around
Cinnamon, say. And such work, if at last
It sees the light of print, is quickly passed
Over with 'What a drag!' So from the start
It goes unread. The Apollonian dart,
Corrosive and austere, has made no sores
Upon these creatures. They are sophomores
In painting or creative writing; no one
Taught them to write, or to put pigment on,
So ink and paint are squandered; both are laid
On so thick, the daub disgusts the trade.
     The other track provides for those who seem
In their sense of themselves, in an extreme
Consumption of the fire. Whatever odd
Sense 'poet' has, they pass it on the nod;
Fed, for their part, on Terror, and the God.

Of these no more than four or five are known
To have existed, mostly Greek. Their tone
Is matter-of-fact and prosy—that's a blind;
Silly old tales on the surface, but behind
A beautiful science. That's the trick of it:
To be, while easy, cryptic. They could profit
In this way by the confident obtuseness
Of their much pampered public, and its less
Than open mind; its eyebrow raised, its jeer
Reserved for arcane verities made clear.
    These first made current whole theodicies
And abstruse astrological expertise,
While camouflaging this, by an astute
Highly developed use of anecdote
From a purblind public. God won't let them be,
His sizzling probe pricks insecurity
Into them always. Men like these are found—
Not without some complacency—'unsound',
Countryside crazies. It's believed they've much
Traffic with fairies (those!), and nymphs, and such.
    Cutting between these two tracks there's a third
Which, since it holds the middle, is preferred
As what God has supposedly designed
To satisfy the appetite in mankind
For culling an elect. This kind supports,
So runs the theory, the performing arts;
It's educational, irrigates the masses.
It spreads civility through evening-classes,
Where sinking selfhood in a common cause
Is a point much stressed. But then, our trip-wire wars
Or (worse) our big-time cosmos-splitters seem
Hardly at all to share a common theme
With Drayton's 'Agincourt'. Belligerent airs
Do wonders for morale, so long as there's
No chance we hear the enemy singing theirs.
So, if it comes to patrons, there's no doubt
Bellona and mad Captain Mars are out.
Which leaves us with the staged, or stagey; not
The happiest prospect . . .
                          Tragic plots are what,

So it was thought, some few great houses foster:
Plantagenet, Gore-Booth, Adams, Malatesta,
Atreus, Thebes. But ritual couplings, treasons,
Condign kills and shames are for all seasons
And all conditions. Thinking of your bog-queen,
Intact, tar-black when disinterred, I've seen
This calls for Comedy, never more demonic
Than when Divine, involved and unironic,
Painful and pitying. (This she also knew,
Your wife, who took the cannibal Ugolino
As type for poets: brain devouring brain,
One 'rabid egotistical daisy-chain'.)
Knowing what's out of joint is our dilemma
In Ireland, Denmark, England, the Maremma;
What is, what isn't. In your singing-school,
Dante's and yours, the dreadful is the rule.
        Dread; yes, dread—the one name for the one
Game that we play here, surely. I think Sisson
Got it, don't you? Plain Dante, plain as a board,
And if flat, flat. The abhorrent, the abhorred,
Ask to be uttered plainly. Heaney, I
Appeal to you who are more in the public eye
Than us old codgers: isn't it the case
The Muse must look disaster in the face?
        Well, but—here comes the compliment, somewhat late
But sent with feeling—none should denigrate
Your early Georgics. None of us would steal
From your tin scoop plunged in a tub of meal
Its pre-Dantesque Homeric virtue. Those
English who prize your verse as rustic prose
Are not all wrong: Agricola is one
Hero persists. Farmer and farmer's son
Are two 'scape whipping. And the traveller,
Odysseus Weather-eye the navigator,
He's another. Both of them you've been,
And lover too; Apollo set the scene
And then these various provocations planned,
Providing that in ancient Ireland and
Historic England Heaney should rehearse
Cottage economies, curtness of good verse.

DEATH OF A VOICE

After Pasternak
and to him

1.

Here is its mark left, thumbnail of enigma.
—It is late, you will sleep, come dawn you will try to read it.
And meanwhile to awaken the loved one, and to touch her
As you may do is given to no other.

How you have touched her! Though your lips were bronze
They touched her, as tragedians touch the stalls.
A kiss there was like summer, hung and hung
And only after that, your sound of thunder.

It drank, as birds drink; took till the senses swooned.
Long, long the stars flowed in from throat to lung.
Nightingales too, their eyes start, as by spasms
Drop by drop they wring night's arches dry.

2.

Dawn will agitate the tapers,
Spark and propel house-martins to their mark.
Admonitory, in you dart:
Let life be always as bran-new as this.

Dawn, like a shot into the dark.
Bang, bang!—the wadding as it flies
Out of the rifle sees its spark go out.
Let life be always as bran-new as this.

Once more, outside—a puff of wind.
What night-long waited on us quivers.
With dawn came rain, and the rain shivers.
Let life be always as bran-new as this.

It is distinctly ludicrous!
Why should it bother with the man on guard?

· It saw its own way in was barred.
Let life be always as bran-new as this.

Give us your orders, now, upon the drop
Of a handkerchief, the while you are still *seigneur*
While, for the while that we are at a loss,
The while, the while the spark's not blown upon!

  3.

In the unparented, insomniac
Damp and universal vast
A volley of groans breaks loose from standing posts,
And still the nightwind, self-aborted, idles.

And hard behind, in an unseeing scurry
Some slant drops fall. About a stretch of fencing
Damp branches quarrel with the pallid wind
Sharply. I quail. You, bone of their contention!

MANDELSTAM'S 'OCTETS'

  66.
I love the way the weave, when two or three or
Four sometimes great gulps can't draw it tight,
Comes up, comes clear; when I achieve a more
Shuddering breath, and get it sounding right.
So much good that does me, yet I fetch
Much weight upon me, as the moment nears
When the arched breastbone, onerously a-stretch
Through my slurred mumblings, signals in your ears.

  67.
I love the way the weave, when two or three or
Four sometimes great gulps can't draw it tight,
Comes up, comes clear; when I achieve a more

Shuddering breath, and get it sounding right.
Meanwhile, by the arch of spinnakers beguiled
To open-form regattas, Space is idling
And adumbrating, half-awake—a child
That's never learned what would be meant by cradling.

68.

When you have shoved aside the scribbled worksheet,
And what you hold in your intent mind is
Contentless, not to be glossed, just one complete
Arc on your inward dark, one sentence's
Periodic structure (eyes screwed shut
Upon itself, on the strength itself supplies)—
This had to do with the page that you will blot
As much as a cupola does, with vacant skies.

69.

Advise me, draftsman of the drifting sands,
Geometer of wilderness, are these
Intractable alignments countermands
More clinching than the wind's voluminous scurries?
—Nothing to me such tremulous demurrers,
Judaic qualms! His baby burble builds
Experience out of babble, burble slurs
Imbibing the experience, modelling it.

70.

Butterfly-girl of the Mussulman, all
In a cut-to-ribbons winding-sheet, who are
Livelong and deathlong, lifeling, deathling, tall
Insectile apparition, this same one
With the immense antennae and her chomping
Head hooded in a burnous, she has strayed
Out, at large. O, the flag of a winding-sheet, please
Furl it, and fold your wings—I am afraid!

71.

Well, but the saw-edged maple-leaf can suffer
To have its claws drawn for it, in some fine
Perfected corner; butterfly-markings offer
Themselves that way, motifs for a mural design.
I have it now, of a sudden:
                                                    mosques there are
That live and persist along with us. In our throes
We are perhaps ourselves Hagia Sophia,
That looks with our eyes out through innumerous windows.

72.

Schubert from water, from birdsong's gamut Mozart;
Goethe, a trill down much-bewildered byways!
Hamlet's balked gait, itself his pensive part—
All took the crowd's pulse, banked on the crowded phrase.
Maybe, before we lipped them, lispings moved;
Where woods were not, already foliage flittered;
And those we propose experience to, have proved
In advance of experience fitted for it, and featured.

73.

Those plaguy, needling games of ours, where stooks
Of jackstraws figure, phials whence we drink
Illusions of causality! These hooks
With which we touch on Quantities, we think,
Are deathly playthings; one small figure catches
On to another as the hook is cast
Over, and snags. The child, though, sleeps. The vast
Universe sleeps, where cradled Eternity watches.

74.

I come in out of Space, and with a rake
In Quantity's garden that can do with tending
Grub up self-knowing Causes and the fake
Invariant there. My one book you, the Unending,
Wrote for me and I read it alone, in seclusion;

It is your leafless, your wayward Guide to Wild Herbs,
It is your book of difficult sums for solving,
Telling of massive roots, the squares, the cubes.

75.

To get past harping on the laws of Nature
The blue-hard eye has pierced to the Law behind:
Lodged in the earth's crust, zany is God's own creature
And upthrust, grubbed from the breast, his groan is mined.
The aborted foetus, deaf, something can bend it;
Like a forge-ahead road it is bowed back, hooped to a horn
—The plenty of bent-in Space, to apprehend it
Takes up the pledge of the petal's, the cupola's form;

76.

And of the sixth sense, the infinitesimal suffix;
Or else the minute sincipital eye of the lizard;
Cloisters of cochlea, cockles, the snail-shell helix;
And the cilia's small-talk, hairline flicker and hazard.
The unattainable, how near it comes!
No disuniting it, no scrutinies—
As with a message pressed into your hand, that is
To have an answer by return, at once!

Note: Of Mandelstam's 'Octets' or 'eight-liners', composed as a whole in
Moscow in 1933 (though incorporating some writing from as late as
July 1935), Clarence Brown has said: 'these poems are in no sense an
isolated statement or a momentary excursus into metaphysics. They
are central to an understanding of Mandelstam . . .' The text I have
worked from is that established by Professor Brown in 'Mandelstam's
Notes Towards a Supreme Fiction', in *Delos* (Austin, Texas, 1968),
Vol. I, no. 1; the order of the poems in the sequence, and accordingly
the numbers given to them, are those of Professor Brown—they have
been printed in another order. In the case of poems so cryptic as these,
translation cannot help but be at the same time interpretation; and I am
greatly indebted to Clarence Brown's commentary (loc. cit.), though I
have dared to differ from him somewhat, and the difference is registered
in my versions. Though it must by no means be supposed that Henry
Gifford approves of this enterprise, I am pleased to acknowledge that
he assisted me crucially at several points.

LADY COCHRANE
Before the House of Lords, 24 July 1862

That honoured name!
    Hero of a hundred fights!
A man who could have ruled
the world upon the sea . . .
    She cannot bear
    to be sitting there
to vindicate the name
for ages and for ages
'has run the World with his deeds'.

Once too often he had fenced
With the Commons, when, incensed,
    Coldly they saw depart
    Their pocket Bonaparte.
Nor would their chiefs, though too obtuse
To recognize in him a loose
    Bold travesty upon
    Cast down Napoleon
(Their fiercer Cromwell, now immured
On St Helena, and secured
    By sloop and spyglass), grieve
    To see rash Cochrane leave.

'Hero of a hundred fights!
I have stood upon the battledeck.
I have seen men fall. I have raised them.
I have fired a gun to save a man.
For the honour of my husband, I would do it again.'

So liberated Chile bought
The impenitent class-traitor out:
    The stormy petrel planes
    Again the ocean-lanes!

'Yes, I did assent
to accompany him to Scotland.'
—What time did you leave London?—
'The evening of the sixth of August
eighteen hundred and twelve.'
—How did you travel? It is
unimportant?—
                'Yes, it is unimportant.'
—With great speed, with four horses?—
'Sometimes, sometimes with two
as we could, night and day.
He named Carlisle and several other towns.
I was tired, worn. I was young.'

Demonic syren-voices choired
From St Helena, as the hired
        Condottiere sailed
        Past impetus that failed.
O'Higgins then, and San Martìn
Await him, in the Alpine, keen
        Air they have burned through, all
        Singed by an Empire's fall.

'A sort of pet name of his own
he had for me, and he said:
"It is all right, Mouse.
Mouse, we are over the Border."
He said: "You are mine for ever."
He snapped his fingers the way
that Scotchmen do
when they are pleased. I arrived
at Annan on the evening of the eighth,
and when I arrived at the Queensberry Arms
he was very joyous; I suppose
men in love are. He said:
"It is all right, it is all right."
He sat himself down as any gentleman might:
"I came here, Dick, to be married
and this is my wife," turning to me; and he bowed.'

Look! Abashed, the Portuguese
Are scoured in one year from the seas:
        So much one man can do
        That does, and knows not how.
Brazil, a Lusitanian mouth,
Can best acclaim, and will, the South
        American Lafayette,
        And pay at last her debt;
And shall she weakly countermand,
To one grown stiffer in command,
        His licence to hold sway
        Who will, at will, obey?
Does genius not inscribe and fill
Time's empty page with eagle's quill?
        So, when the albatross
        Has fished, and sailed across
One mast and tossing ensign, will
The flag direct him where to kill
        Next, in the self-sought, clear
        Taut arc of his career?

'After the paper was signed
and the servants gone, he began
to dance the Sailor's Hornpipe.
He put his hands up, so,
and "Now you are mine," he said.
—You marry like this in Scotland?—
"Oh yes," he said, "you are mine.
I have no time to spare, I have no time to lose."
He kissed me, he did not go
into my room, and he went off as he came.'

—I understand your ladyship
to say it was in order
not to displease his Uncle,
from whom he had expectations,
he kept his marriage a secret?—
'Entirely so. By a secret
marriage he would avoid
this fortune going away.'

Still voluble, still undeterred,
Our Cochranes keep their cloudy word:
      The same arts that did gain
      Them power, their power maintain,
Though thou, the war's and Fortune's son,
Terse Napoleon, bend upon
      Play-acting pitched so high
      A veiled, sardonic eye.

'The old lady there, in the house
spoke a very broad Scotch. I never
heard Scotch before. I said
(I was but young you know,
perhaps a little pert) . . .
I said: "What kind of place
do you call this?"
             She said:
"The Queensberry Arms at Annan." '

'I have stood on the battledeck . . .
I would do it again . . .' the voice
defensive and defiant.

TO LONDONERS

I get, surprisingly, a sense of space:
As on the rush-hour underground, when in fact
Every one touches, still in his own place
Every one rises above the smirch of contact,
Resolute to assert his self-containment;
A charged field cordons every sovereign will.

The City empty on a July evening,
All the jam-packed commuters gone, and all
The Wren and Hawksmoor spires and steeples shining
In a honeyed light . . . But also mental spaces
As I see now, all energies withdrawn
To hold the frontiers each day menaces.

Trying to hold my own place just inside
The emptied space round Hawksmoor's drawing-board,
I shoulder, I am rancorous, I have tried
Too long, with too much vigour and the wrong
Sort of patience. On the District Line
Budge up a little, tell me I belong!

Gallant baritones whom nothing soured
Between the wars, still hooked on Rupert Brooke
Who adumbrated for the earlier war
A wide and windy Iliad in the embowered
Old garden of the Vicarage, Grantchester . . .
Is that the bugle-note you listen for?

Given a voice thus confident, thus confiding,
As intimate as a commuter's week
And yet as sweeping as imperial war
Or global peace, how spaciously I could
Bind in one *sostenuto* Temple Bar
With Turnham Green, St Paul's with Chorleywood!

But now or later you will have to say
I am one of yours. Do you not hear the cramp
Of overpopulation, of *mêlée*
In this too tamped-down, pounded-together ramp
Of phrases I manhandle towards what yawning
Yard of what temple, what too void arena?